50 things you can do today to manage

stress at work

Professor Cary Cooper
Dr Howard Kahn

PERSONAL HEALTH GUIDES

summersdale

50 THINGS YOU CAN DO TODAY TO MANAGE STRESS AT WORK

Summersdale Publishers Ltd
46 West Street
Chichester
West Sussex
PO19 1RP
UK

www.summersdale.com

Printed and bound by CPI Group (UK) Ltd, Croydon, CR0 4YY

ISBN: 978-1-84953-342-3

Substantial discounts on bulk quantities of Summersdale books are available to corporations, professional associations and other organisations. For details contact Nicky Douglas by telephone: +44 (0) 1243 756902, fax: +44 (0) 1243 786300 or email: nicky@summersdale.com.

Disclaimer
Every effort has been made to ensure that the information in this book is accurate and current at the time of publication. The author and the publisher cannot accept responsibility for any misuse or misunderstanding of any information contained herein, or any loss, damage or injury, be it health, financial or otherwise, suffered by any individual or group acting upon or relying on information contained herein. None of the opinions or suggestions in this book is intended to replace medical opinion. If you have concerns about your health, please seek professional advice.

To my grandchildren Jai and Isabella, who I hope will manage stress better than I did when I was young!
(Cary)

To my wife Valerie and our daughter Jacqueline, hoping that they will not be stressed by anything at work or home.
(Howard)

Acknowledgements

To all my former PhD students who supported me
and kept me stress free, including Howard!
(Cary)

To Valerie, my wife, and Jacqueline, my
daughter, and to Ray and Marjorie –
they know about stress at work.
(Howard)

Other titles in the Personal Health Guides series include:

50 Things You Can Do Today to Manage Stress

50 Things You Can Do Today to Increase Your Fertility

50 Things You Can Do Today to Manage Arthritis

50 Things You Can Do Today to Manage Back Pain

50 Things You Can Do Today to Manage Eczema

50 Things You Can Do Today to Manage Fibromyalgia

50 Things You Can Do Today to Manage Hay Fever

50 Things You Can Do Today to Manage IBS

50 Things You Can Do Today to Manage Insomnia

50 Things You Can Do Today to Manage Migraines

50 Things You Can Do Today to Manage Menopause

Contents

Authors' Note

When I was working as a social worker in downtown Los Angeles, I worked with underprivileged black people in South Central LA district and with the poor and homeless in the city centre. I saw real poverty and deprivation, but most of all I saw the daily grind and stress in people's lives. For most, they didn't have the coping strategies to deal with the enormous financial, social and psychological problems they faced. This had a lasting impact on me from that moment on. While I was working as a social worker, I was also studying for my MBA, and I decided that being an accountant or corporate lawyer was not going to be a personally fulfilling career for me, that I wanted to make some kind of difference in people's lives. I then modified my course to concentrate on organisational psychology and behavioural science, and moved gradually into workplace health and occupational stress. Slowly and gradually this led me inevitably to researching what work does to people, how it stresses them and/or enhances their wellbeing and health. I have since then carried out research on a variety of occupations, from teachers to pilots to women managers to doctors to international interpreters. It is this collective wisdom, developed over the years with dozens of my PhD students that this book is based on. I am pleased to say that Howard Kahn was one of these students, who ended up a friend and valued colleague over the years, and without whom I could not have done this book.

Professor Cary Cooper

I first became familiar with stress when I worked in the City of London beside those who buy and sell currency, Eurobonds, gilts, and trade in stocks, fixed institutional sales, swaps, and so on. They were (and still are) well paid, but suffered from a great deal of stress. As a result they consumed much alcohol, indulged in dangerous behaviours, and were 'burnt-out' by the time they were in their late 30s. I asked myself what I could do to help them. Since then, I have been working with people in more 'ordinary' occupations, and it is clear that many of them are stressed by the situation they find themselves in at work. The aim of this book is to help people who suffer stress at work, which, in an era of globalisation, redundancies, longer hours, and concerns about the future, is becoming more stressful than ever.

Dr Howard Kahn

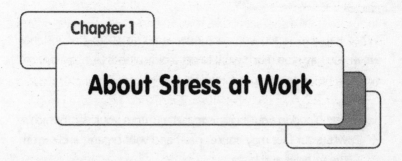

Chapter 1

About Stress at Work

Do you suffer from stress at work? Don't worry – you're not alone. The International Labour Organization, based in Geneva, Switzerland, has been concerned about work-related stress for many years and claims it is one of the most important issues in many countries and in different kinds of workplaces. The outcomes of stress can include circulatory and gastrointestinal diseases, other physical problems, psychosomatic and psychosocial problems, and low productivity. At an organisational level, the UK Chartered Institute of Personnel and Development estimates stress costs industry £601 per employee.

The purpose of this book is to help you realise the actions you can take to manage and control stress at work, both from an individual and management point of view. The book will also explain the methods you can use to cope with stress at work – such as deep breathing or exercise – and will show you how to change the circumstances (whether at work or not) that may be causing your stress.

The first thing we will do is show what stress is and the major causes of stress at work. We will then suggest what you can do – as an individual, supervisor or manager – to deal with these issues. In some cases we will also show how the stress can arise.

What is stress?

What happens when you are under stress at work (for instance when you have too much work to do, a difficult boss, unpleasant co-workers, no prospects for promotion, fear of losing your job, etc.)?

 The blood in your body is redirected from your skin (which is why your face may appear pale) and your organs, and sent to the muscles and brain.

 The glucose and fatty acids you naturally have stored in your body are transferred into your bloodstream so you will have energy to deal with the threat you are under.

You become much more alert – your hearing and vision are greatly improved.

Your immune system is weakened.

Overall, chemicals such as adrenaline are produced, your heart rate goes up, your blood vessels dilate, your breathing becomes faster, you sweat more, your metabolism slows down, and the production of oestrogen, androgen and other sex hormones are reduced.

This is all done to prepare the body for 'fight or flight', that is, to get ready to cope with the problem causing your stress, by either dealing with it or running away from it. Once you have dealt with the problem, your body will return to normal. But what if you can't deal with the problem? What if the problem continues day after day? The many changes in your body continue and you can end up with the problems outlined above – and more.

The short-term outcomes of stress

Mind, the UK mental health charity, has listed the signs associated with experiencing too much stress and has divided them into three groups – how your body may react, how you may feel and how you may behave.

How your body may react:

 Fast shallow breathing

 Headaches

 Constant tiredness

 Restlessness

 Sleeping problems

 Tendency to sweat

 Nervous twitches

 Craving for food

 Cramps or muscle spasms

Pins and needles

High blood pressure

Feeling sick or dizzy

 Constipation or diarrhoea

 Indigestion or heartburn

 Lack of appetite

 Sexual difficulties

 Fainting

 Chest pains

 Grinding your teeth at night

How you may feel:

 Irritable

 Aggressive

Depressed

Fearing failure

Dreading the future

A loss of interest in others

Taking no interest in life

Neglected

 That there's no one to confide in

 A loss of sense of humour

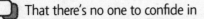 Bad or ugly

 Fearful that you are seriously ill

How you may behave:

 Finding it difficult to make decisions

 Finding it difficult to concentrate

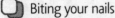 Denying there's a problem

 Avoiding difficult situations

 Frequently crying

Biting your nails

Unable to show your true feelings

Being very snappy or aggressive

Finding it difficult to talk to others

Mind suggests that the more of these you experience, the more stressed you are.

What are the organisational outcomes of stress at work?

We have described how stress can affect you as an individual, but what happens to an organisation when its staff are suffering from too much stress? It can suffer reduced productivity caused by, among other things:

 A higher turnover of staff

 Staff coming to work late and leaving early

 Staff sitting about doing nothing

 A poor reputation (because the organisation is known as one that causes stress for their employees)

 Higher levels of staff absenteeism

 Poorer quality of work

 More workplace accidents

 More strikes

Law cases brought against the organisation by those suffering from stress.

What are the sources of stress at work?

Of course, almost anything at work can cause stress to someone. Some people are in a permanent state of anxiety and the smallest thing might stress them out. You might spot them in your workplace, but their problems are beyond the scope of this book. They need help to change the way they think and behave. What we are concerned with here are the major sources of stress at work, the things that cause you stress, and what you can do about them.

How do we know what causes stress at work?

A large number of studies of different workplaces have been carried out over the past 50 years to determine the major sources of stress at work. For instance, studies have focused on NHS employees and other medical staff, City of London dealers, teachers and university lecturers, bus drivers, office workers, company directors, middle managers, public and private employees, etc.

There has been general agreement about the sources of stress: no matter what the organisation, the major causes are similar. There appear to be five major sources of stress at work:

1. The stressors that come with the job, such as your working conditions, the technology you have to work with, the work itself – sometimes an overload of work, sometimes an underload – or working long hours.

2. The role of the individual – whether this involves role conflict or role ambiguity – and the responsibility you have for others.

3. Your career development. Perhaps you feel you are not being challenged in your current role, or you consider yourself worthy of a promotion due to a large workload. Perhaps you are worried

about your job security in relation to mergers and acquisitions that could affect your organisation. The relationships you have with others at work – with your boss, colleagues, clients and customers.

4. The organisational climate and culture – what it's like to work for the organisation, the office politics, communication, the participation you have in the decision-making process, any restrictions on your behaviour (dress code, no smoking allowed, etc.), performance appraisals, and so on.

5. Your work–life balance. This category of potential stressors consists of events outside work that affect you at work. These include life events (moving house, getting married, deaths and illnesses in the family, etc.), and dual-career families (where both partners are working).

These seem to be the factors that cause the most stress at work. Don't forget that everyone is different and some people have personalities that deflect or attract stress. These characteristics include anxiety (a tendency to worry about events and people, and the strength of that worry); neuroticism (that is, the tendency to experience negative emotional states such as anger, envy, guilt and depression); a tolerance for ambiguity (an ability to cope with things that are uncertain and unpredictable); and whether you are a Type A person (ambitious, organised, taking on too much work, obsessed with time management, etc.).

The level of stress you experience is also determined by the strategies you use to cope with stress. These can be personal strategies or the organisation you work for may help you to deal with any stress you encounter.

If we put together all the points raised above, we can show you a model of stress at work (see the diagram below). This is based on the model developed by Cary Cooper and Judi Marshall.

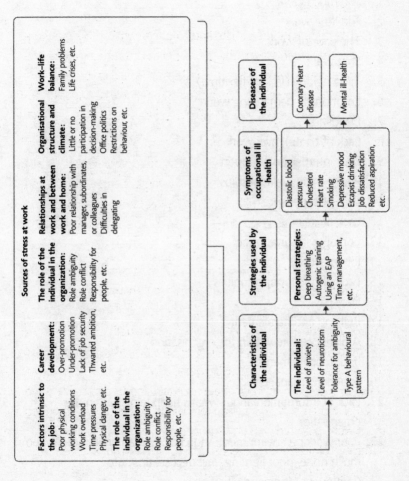

Sources of stress at work

Factors intrinsic to the job:
Poor physical working conditions
Work overload
Time pressures
Physical danger, etc.

The role of the individual in the organization:
Role ambiguity
Role conflict
Responsibility for people, etc.

Career development:
Over-promotion
Under-promotion
Lack of job security
Thwarted ambition, etc.

The role of the individual in the organization:
Role ambiguity
Role conflict
Responsibility for people, etc.

Relationships at work and between work and home:
Poor relationship with manager, subordinates, or colleagues
Difficulties in delegating

Organisational structure and climate:
Little or no participation in decision-making
Office politics
Restrictions on behaviour, etc.

Work-life balance:
Family problems
Life crises, etc.

Characteristics of the individual

The individual:
Level of anxiety
Level of neuroticism
Tolerance for ambiguity
Type A behavioural pattern

Strategies used by the individual

Personal strategies:
Deep breathing
Autogenic training
Using an EAP
Time management, etc.

Symptoms of occupational ill health

Diastolic blood pressure
Cholesterol
Heart rate
Smoking
Depressive mood
Escapist drinking
Job dissatisfaction
Reduced aspiration, etc.

Diseases of the individual

Coronary heart disease

Mental ill-health

The 50 most-quoted causes of stress at work

1. Too much work
2. Too little work
3. The pace of work
4. Shift work
5. Time rigidity (lack of flexitime)
6. Emotionally demanding work
7. Deadlines
8. Lack of control over work
9. Poor interpersonal support
10. Poor working relationships
11. Lack of experience
12. Lack of training
13. Coping with promotion
14. Job insecurity
15. Lack of career opportunities
16. Poor pay
17. Bullying and harassment
18. A blame culture within the organisation
19. Poor management
20. Too many managers
21. Lack of information about what's happening within the organisation
22. Poor working environment – too hot/cold an environment, too much noise, poor lighting, incorrect seating, etc.
23. Continuous lifting and vibration
24. Malfunctioning equipment
25. Conflict
26. Constant change
27. Role ambiguity

28. Role conflict
29. Personal life affecting work
30. Work affecting personal life
31. Unreliable performance reviews (and positive reviews that do not lead to a pay rise)
32. Lack of money
33. Overtime (especially at the weekends)
34. Little or no time to rest and recover
35. Commuting
36. Organisational culture
37. Lack of power and influence
38. Doing a job that you are over-qualified or under-qualified for
39. Supervising other people
40. Depending on other team members/colleagues
41. Office politics
42. Personal beliefs conflicting with those of the organisation
43. Doing a job others disapprove of
44. Keeping up with new technology
45. Attending meetings
46. Covert discrimination and favouritism
47. Inability to delegate
48. Too little or too much variety in the job
49. Organisational commitment
50. Sacking others

The remainder of this book is concerned with how to deal with these sources of stress at work. In some cases we indicate why the stressor arises in some organisations, what the typical effects of the stress are and what you can do about it. We will suggest the most important things you can do to manage the sources of stress at work – today.

For further reading about stress, see *50 Things You Can Do Today To Manage Stress* by Wendy Green, which explains the psychological and lifestyle factors that can contribute to stress, and offers practical advice and a holistic approach to help you deal with its symptoms, as well as dietary and lifestyle changes and complementary therapies.

Chapter 2

The Job Itself

1. How to cope when you have too much work to do

There can be no doubt that constantly having too much work to do will cause stress – various studies have shown this. For instance, an investigation into members of a white-collar union employed in drafting, mechanical and technical-clerical jobs in a manufacturing company showed that having too much work resulted in job dissatisfaction, fatigue and tension. A study into nurses and nursing assistants found that among the main source of stress for nurses was having too much work to do. Too much work can also result in interference with personal life. An examination of managers concluded that a large proportion of those in a typical production environment appeared at risk of developing psychological illness because they took on so much work.

A study in the *American Sociological Review* found that mothers spend ten more hours a week multitasking compared with fathers. These additional hours are mainly related to time spent on housework and childcare, and this can result in an increase in negative emotions, stress, psychological distress and work–family conflict. (By contrast, fathers' multitasking at home was not a negative experience!) Community and hospital pharmacists in Northern Ireland found an excessive workload to be among the most stressful aspects of their employment.

How does it happen?

 Your boss can't say 'no' to their boss.

 Your organisation is short-staffed.

 Deadlines are shifted.

 You feel you have to work harder and longer to keep your job.

Your manager has no idea how much work you have to do.

How do you know when you have too much work to do?

 You make more mistakes.

 You become short-tempered with other people at work and at home.

You become less efficient at work.

 You work late in an effort to keep up with the work.

You bring work home with you.

What can you do about it?

Ask your boss what your priorities are and reschedule your work accordingly. The less important elements of your work can wait or be given to someone else. The best way to prioritise your work is to divide your tasks into four categories: first, important and urgent tasks, which MUST be done; second, tasks that are important but not urgent (make sure you allocate enough time to do these because they are often left to one side); third, tasks that are urgent but not important (these are often tasks that are given to you by your boss – you know they are not important but you still have to complete them); fourth, tasks that are not important and not urgent (such as people interrupting you).

Approach other people, especially if you work in a team, and ask if they can take on some of your work (don't forget you'll probably have to pay back the debt in the future).

Recruit other people and/or outsource (if you can).

Say no to requests to do additional work. Very often the inability to say no causes stress. The best way to say no is to say something like 'Sorry, I can't do it at this moment'. Or you might say you'll get back to them and, when you do, say you've looked at your schedule and you can't find time to fit in the extra work. Or, if you want, you can tell them you're able to take on part of the extra work, but not all of it, as you're so busy.

Avoid interruptions – lock your door. Return phone calls, emails and text messages at specific times. At other times, let your voicemail take messages for you and set up an email auto-reply letting people know when you will respond.

 Do the difficult jobs first. If you do the easy ones first you may spend more time than you think getting them right.

Set goals for the day. Schedule your time to include interruptions.

Delegate (if you can).

Do not try to achieve perfection. If you do, you'll find you spend far more time than the work requires, and the task you're doing becomes much bigger and more important than it deserves. Of course, some jobs DO require perfection – like a surgeon or an accountant.

2. How to cope when you have too little work to do

You might think having too little work to do would be great, but not having enough to do can affect your psychological well-being. Quantitative underload (having too little work to do) leads to what has been called 'rust out', and to boredom and apathy. This can lead to inattentiveness, which ultimately can be dangerous. For example, work underload in crane drivers has been found to be a significant source of stress. These drivers can get bored and inattentive, and do not follow the operations manual relating to the crane. They take chances. Qualitative underload (when you're not given an opportunity to use your skills and abilities or you have a routine, repetitive job that results in lack of mental stimulation) also leads to 'rust out', and is very obvious in new graduate recruits, who start their first full-time job and find their high expectations are not met. This leads to job dissatisfaction and lower motivation. In a study of male and female blue-collar workers it has been found that that work underload resulted in men having an increased systolic blood pressure (when the heart is contracting). For women, however, work underload resulted in higher cholesterol.

How does it happen?

○ You do not have the skills needed to do the work, so it is not given to you.

○ There are peaks and troughs when it comes to work volume – now is a trough.

○ Work has been outsourced (and this may result in you having insufficient work to fill your time).

○ Your reputation for completing the work is poor, so you are not given any.

○ Your boss or colleagues cannot delegate – they do the work themselves.

○ There are no new projects or business to be dealt with.

○ You are in the wrong job.

You are underutilised.

What happens to you?

 You are bored and apathetic at work.

 The quality of your work is poor.

 You do your work half-heartedly.

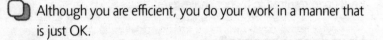 Although you are efficient, you do your work in a manner that is just OK.

You do your work, but you do not feel you have ownership of the final product – this may result in you feeling dissatisfied.

What can you do about it?

If you know that the work you are required to do is too demanding for you, or you need more training to complete it, you should consider either going on a training course (if one is available), or opting to self-educate yourself to have the opportunity to realise new possibilities.

Offer to mentor other employees – especially new ones. This will show your organisation you care about the progress of individuals and that you care about the company's future. Studies have shown that mentors and those mentored achieve a higher job satisfaction, which in turn leads to increased productivity and reduced staff turnover.

Talk to your boss/colleagues and tell them you can take on some of their work. This will show you are able to do more than your current workload.

 Do work that has been lying about for some time and no one has tackled.

 Become a union representative. You will learn a great deal about the company you are working for and the people employed there. But remember, a recent survey showed that almost all union representatives think their career prospects have been damaged by their personal involvement with unions.

 Ask for a transfer to another group/department.

Help at home

Don't be afraid to ask for help at home. If you are overloaded at work, ask your partner to help with your household chores until your workload is under control. If you have work underload, make an effort to keep your home life busy and stimulating; take up a new hobby or tackle a project you have been avoiding.

3. How to keep up with the pace of work

Work pace is concerned with who, or what, decides the pace of work to be done. The European Working Conditions Observatory noted in 2009 that the 'drivers' of work pace and stress at work were customers/clients, managers, colleagues, deadlines, routines and machinery, and that in recent years the importance of customers/clients has increased and is currently a major factor influencing the pace of work. It also suggested that these changes can expose employees to situations where they are attempting to fulfil customers'/clients' endless demands under circumstances where they get little support. Therefore, the possibility of an increase – sometimes sudden, sometimes regular – in work pace, is typical of the modern workplace.

Also, many workers nowadays spend all their time in front of a computer and, despite knowing they should take a break in order to rest their eyes, wrists and minds, continue to work, driven on by the never-ending demands of the computer. Perhaps you are one of these – this might result in you fainting because you suddenly stand up after sitting in the same position for a long time!

How does it happen?

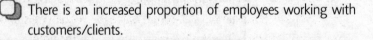 There is an increased proportion of employees working with customers/clients.

Managers now want organisations to be customer oriented, staff numbers reduced, and authority and decision-making decentralised – all of which can add to the pressure on employees.

Staff demand greater responsibility, freedom at work and personal development, and this has been reflected by support at the policy and legislative level. This in itself can result in more demands being made on the employee.

 The speed of operation and production is determined by a source other than the employee.

How do you know when you cannot cope with the pace of work you are expected to maintain?

 You suffer from repetitive strain injury.

 You have no time to relax and rest at work.

You have no control over the pace of an assembly line or the demands made on you.

You are doing a job that has low-decision latitude (you have little ability to decide how you do your job) combined with low social support (you feel you are not cared for by other people).

 You are being monitored and are required to work at a constant, fast pace. For example, call-centre managers require calls to be completed by call-centre workers within a specific time.

What can you do about it?

Arrange for you and your manager to have a discussion about the pace of work – you could tell your manager that if the pace is too fast, quality will suffer. This should only be done if you genuinely feel you and your co-workers are operating at a pace that is too fast. If you are the only person struggling you must question if you fit the job role. There are some rules you must follow if you want to negotiate this (or anything else at work). Make sure you know what you want from the negotiations; don't get angry with the other person, keep calm and show concern for and understanding of the other person's point of view; choose the right time to start negotiations (not when your boss is busy or in a bad mood); ensure that both you and the other party get something from the negotiations. To negotiate successfully you may have to improve your communication skills, both verbal and non-verbal.

Have regular rest breaks at work and use some activities that can help you relieve stress, such as stretching, walking about, improving your breathing, or repeating a word to yourself (a mantra), like 'relax'.

Tell your boss there is evidence that employees who can control the pace of their work suffer from less stress than those who cannot control the pace of their work. Employees who can control this are off work for less time and staff turnover is lower.

You may have to face up to the fact that you are not able to deal with a fast-paced job, and you should consider whether or not it is time to change to a job with low demands or to one that provides you with higher control.

4. How to deal with shift work

Many organisations need to be available to their clients 24 hours a day, for example, the fire, police and ambulance services, hospitals and public utilities, etc. To achieve this they may well have to use shift workers. There are at least 3.6 million shift workers in the UK and there are many different shift patterns. One researcher in the USA has reported 487 different shift work patterns. Shift work can be 'continuous' (working at weekends) or 'discontinuous' (working Monday to Friday only). Although some people are always on night shifts, others work different shifts that rotate weekly or monthly. They may also have to work 10- or 12-hour shifts.

The evidence shows that working shifts can cause stress. This is because your circadian rhythms fall out of sync with the norm. You usually expect to sleep when it's dark, eat in the morning, at midday and at night, and the metabolism, temperature and hormones of your body react to the time of day. When you have to work shifts, these are thrown out of phase.

When a study of 827 employees working in a manufacturing plant was carried out, results suggested that shift workers suffer from more physical and psychological distresses, sleep problems and stress than non-shift workers. In a study of young female nurses in 11 hospitals, results indicated that in shift-work systems, sufficient sleep hours are needed for nurses who work night shifts to ensure good quality of sleep and, consequently, better services for patients.

Overall, night shift workers report poorer health, as well as lower job satisfaction and increased absenteeism, than day workers. Gastrointestinal disorders are the most prevalent health problems associated with shift and night work. Shift work is associated with an increased risk of major disease (heart disease and cancer) and, of particular concern to pregnant women, results by one researcher suggested that fixed night work during pregnancy increases the risk of late foetal loss.

How does it happen?

 Your organisation's service needs to be available to customers/clients 24 hours a day.

 Your organisation takes on a large, production order.

 The only way you can get computer time (during a computer implementation, for instance) is to come in to work out of hours.

 Your organisation needs to increase production and shift work is the only way to achieve it.

 Deadlines mean your organisation must introduce shift work.

How do you know when you cannot cope with shift work?

 You face a lot of pressures at home, such as looking after your children, taking them to school or the doctor/dentist; staying in for a delivery/gas engineer.

 You miss out on a lot of social activities.

You suffer from chronic sleep reduction and sleeplessness.

◯ You are at your best in the morning and your performance on shifts is poorer.

◯ You are drinking too much alcohol, taking too many headache tablets or smoking too much.

What can you do about it?

Shift work is normally determined by your manager or boss, so make them aware of the facts – shift work schedules should be designed so that they are based around circadian rhythms; employee shift schedules should be rotated in a forward manner (that is, days, then nights, then evenings, then days, nights, etc.); rapidly rotating shifts are better than slow-rotating shifts; a flexible work pattern (for instance, a day off after a run of night-shift work, or starting at 7 a.m. rather than 6 a.m.) is desirable; and employees should be allowed to opt for shift work if they want to.

If you are on shift work, you should make sure you take all available breaks and try to find ways to relax during breaks using gentle exercise, meditation, breathing exercises, etc. You should also maintain a proper diet and eating pattern, eating regularly at the same time, eating light and healthy foods, being careful about your intake of caffeine, alcohol and salt, and avoiding sleeping pills. Sleeping should be done at the same time each day, and you should make the sleeping environment as dark and quiet as possible.

Don't forget that shift work has advantages – shops you visit are quieter; you can go to events that are held during the day; there is often a more relaxed atmosphere at work due to less supervision on night shifts; you can dress more casually; and you tend to form a much stronger bond with your fellow shift workers because there are fewer of you.

> ### Take a break
>
> Set reminders for yourself to take a break from your computer. This can help prevent repetitive strain injury and give you an opportunity to rest during your fast-paced day. You can download free software, such as Workrave (www.workrave.org) that will remind you when it is time to take a break, and time you, so that you stay on schedule.

5. How to deal with deadlines

Some deadlines are non-negotiable. For instance, you may have to deliver a piece of work at a certain time to fit in with another colleague or team as the other group is waiting for you to complete a project before they can proceed. On the other hand, some deadlines are negotiable and can be allowed to slip. In general, though, deadlines can cause stress if you do not know how to deal with them. Stress can either be caused by deadlines or it can affect deadlines – or both. The outcomes of the stress that deadlines cause can include anything we've mentioned previously.

If you are working for yourself as a consultant you should take note of these words by Amrit Hallan (www.freelancefolder.com/how-to-meet-deadlines-and-boost-performance): 'Although some people think that deadlines kill creativity and hamper productivity, they can really help you streamline your energies and focus on the work at hand, especially when you work as a freelancer and have multiple projects to handle. If you don't set deadlines for your individual projects you will soon lose track of time and will never be able to deliver the projects on time to your clients, creating a bad professional reputation in the process. If you want to be taken seriously by your past, present and future clients, you have to take your deadlines seriously and respect them; when you respect your deadlines it means you respect your client's time and also your own time.'

How does it happen?

Your organisation is downsizing, restructuring and outsourcing, etc., and reducing its delivery time to customers and clients. There are fewer staff employed by the organisation. Consequently, deadlines are shrinking.

You do work where set deadlines are the norm.

How do you know when you cannot cope with deadlines?

You panic every time you are given a deadline to meet.

You let things slip so that you are unable to meet the original deadline.

What can you do about it?

If a piece of work is being discussed and you are given the job to do, make sure you have enough time to do the work. Tell your manager what you can feasibly do. Say that you could do A, B and C in the time available, but if they want you to do D as well you'll need more time.

Add extra time to cover all eventualities (they will happen).

Ask your boss for an extension. If you absolutely cannot make the deadline you should contact them and negotiate a second deadline. It's much better to do this than to let the deadline go by without any communication. If you do this, you should show your boss a document that maps out how many hours you work in a day and how long you estimate it will take to complete the task in question.

Get help from your colleagues. You may find that your boss is quite happy with this arrangement – indeed, your boss may suggest this anyway.

Break the work down into manageable pieces. Every project can be reduced to manageable elements. To do this you should take a piece of paper and list the activities you have to do to complete the work. Then, place the activities in the order they must be done. As American author and motivational speaker Richard Carlson said: 'Don't sweat the small stuff' – in other words, don't spend your energy doing little things. Give deadlines to each activity. Build into the deadlines time delays caused by changes to the work, illnesses of key personnel, non-delivery of needed items, etc. Construct a timetable for yourself that indicates what you plan to, or must, complete every day. Or you might prepare a to-do list where you can list those jobs that are playing on your mind. Then just do the work! It may be easier than you think. Sometimes, all it takes is to crack on with the job in hand, even when you have been putting it off as you perceive it to be too hard and too time consuming. Perhaps the work is easier than you thought, other people's expectations were lower than you thought or your worries are greater than you thought. Reward yourself if and when you achieve something – you might take a holiday, have a massage (good for relieving stress) or go out for a meal.

If you miss a deadline, work out what went wrong so you can learn from your mistakes. Also, you need to work out how to deal with the aftermath of a missed deadline: notify the client (who could be within or external to your organisation), apologise, determine what went wrong, inform your client what you will do now and ensure that it doesn't happen again.

6. What to do if your computer at work is making you stressed

Does your computer make you angry? Do you sometimes feel you want to strike it? Every modern organisation depends on its computer systems – without them they would not be able to operate at maximum or any reasonable capacity. You know that your computer is important to the company and you may have to sit in front of it every day – but using it can cause you lots of physical and psychological problems. Some of the negative physical effects can be painful wrists and sore shoulders, and a generally distressed body; the psychological problems include anxiety that the computer will break down, worry that you don't know what's happening, shouting at the machine, etc.

A survey concluded that continually crashing computers, slow load times and annoying technical support are creating an epidemic of a condition called 'Computer Stress Syndrome'. Computer users face a continuous state of anxiety and challenge when they are setting up new computer products, keeping up with software upgrades, and migrating to new applications and operating systems, as well as dealing with malware infections, web threats, identity theft and more.

Some older employees find it difficult to use their computer and this itself can be stressful – younger people have grown up with this technology and they know how it works, what it can do and how to do it. In one test, it was suggested that the same mental demands put upon young and elderly women resulted in different outcomes – mentally demanding computer tasks had a more negative effect on the muscles of the older women than on the young. Older women, it was thought, compensated for age-related changes by reducing their work speed markedly.

How does it happen?

 You are given a computer on your (unsuitable) desk, with your ill-fitting chair, facing the window, etc.

 You are given minimal training.

The computer is very slow.

Your computer takes a long time to load up.

The computer you use is continually crashing.

You constantly worry about the computer catching a virus.

How do you know if your work computer is causing you stress?

You suffer from dry eyes, red eyes, pain in or around the eyes, migraines, etc.

The office environment, such as lighting, reflections, glare, etc., is a major problem when using the computer.

You are stressed out by the number of emails you receive and feel you have to answer them all very quickly.

You feel you must respond to your tweets and social networking messages immediately.

Every time you use the computer you are filled with dread that it will not do what you want.

What can you do about it?

Make sure that your equipment – your desk and chair, etc.– is as comfortable as possible. Your employer may have a legal requirement to meet your needs and help you to use your computer efficiently. If your supervisor won't help you should approach your human resources department and ask for a suitable chair, footrest, handrest, etc.

You can place certain plants at your workstation. These will help with computer stress relief. NASA has recommended English ivy, spider plants and fig trees.

◯ Take regular breaks. Every hour or so, get up from your chair and stretch, or go out into the fresh air if you can.

◯ Ask for help if there is something you cannot do or an error occurs.

◯ Blink your eyes frequently and use eye drops if necessary.

◯ Learn the basic skills you need to deal with stress, such as improving your breathing, relaxing your muscles and laughing.

◯ Prioritise your work (see point 5 How to deal with deadlines).

◯ Backup your work OFTEN. If you're worried about losing all the work you've done, backup your work on an external USB device and you'll still have your data. It makes sense and you'll suffer less stress.

De-clutter your desk

Make sure your workspace surroundings aren't adding to your computer stress. Assess the items you have on your desk and remove any that are unnecessary. Keep stationery and other necessities in a pot or desk tidy. Sort through your paperwork, filing or binning anything that is complete or out-of-date. This will avoid the illusion that you have tasks to be completed and create a spacious environment.

7. How to remain calm when your computer malfunctions

Most of what we do at work, especially in an office, is based on the computer. Many people now do their work at home on a computer, and others work at home as well as in the workplace. Where, when and how we work is being revolutionised – with email, voicemail, mobile phones, laptops, video conferencing, etc. The distinction between work and personal life has become blurred, and we can now find ourselves available round the clock. If you work at home you can lose contact with other humans.

Remember that computers are simply machines: they don't have feelings and they do not respond to your shouting or cajoling. They will do exactly what you have asked them to do but, since computers are machines, they will break down sometimes.

In the modern workplace you have to deal with emails, the phone ringing, your colleagues interrupting your work, etc. You can't do everything well, so prioritise your work. Don't spend all your time on Facebook or Twitter!

Does your computer make you stressed? Take a test to find out. The Computer Hassles Scale was developed by Professor Richard A. Hudiburg of the University of North Alabama and is a 37-item scale. You'll find a copy of it at www.blog.johnjosephbachir.org/2007/06/26/computer-hassles-scale-a-measure-of-computer-stress.

Look at your results. This will give you an idea of what is causing you hassle. The minor irritations we suffer every day are called hassles, such as misplacing our car keys, getting stuck in traffic jams, having minor arguments with our family or colleagues, etc. It is daily hassles, rather than a death in the family, changing jobs, getting married or divorced, that affect us the most. These major events don't occur every day, but hassles do. They happen every day and negatively affect our health.

What can you do about it?

 Backup your work frequently.

 Get answers to your technological problems from the computer itself, via Microsoft, Google, etc.

Take a deep breath or a long walk.

Take a break; don't sit in front of the computer for hours at a time. If you're working at home stretch your legs and your eyes.

8. How to make attending meetings less stressful

Meetings are a fact of life and not just in organisations. They occur everywhere: in social clubs, voluntary organisations, groups of friends, families, etc. – all have meetings. At work there are lots of meetings of groups, departments, teams working on a project, and so on. For some people going to a meeting is a stressful, anxious, boring, time-wasting experience; they'd rather get on with their work.

Why hold meetings in the first place? An effective meeting can serve lots of purposes. But if you spend a lot of your time attending meetings that are a waste of time, you delay achieving your objectives, and consequently may be regarded by others as a poor employee. Some people get fed up in meetings – often the agenda seems to be too long, there are too many people there, you don't make any decisions on important points and it's the same people who contribute at every meeting.

If you dislike meetings, it may be that you are on a different 'schedule' from your boss. It has been speculated that there are two types of schedule: the manager's schedule and the maker's schedule – and most powerful people are on the manager's schedule. However, if you are on the maker's schedule, a meeting can disrupt what you are trying to achieve. Those on the manager's schedule think about what they are doing after the meeting – they think in one-hour chunks. Those on the maker's schedule, who have to spend a morning or afternoon at a meeting, must change the way they think and behave, and that doesn't help when they have to return to work.

Don't forget your bosses. A recent study of how chief executives manage their time found that they spent about a third of their working week in meetings – about 18 hours a week on average. According to *The Wall Street Journal*, American managers spend about a third of their working week in meetings and could save 80 per cent of their wasted time if they started and finished meetings on time, and followed an agenda.

How does it happen?

 You are called to a scheduled meeting.

You are called to an unscheduled meeting.

An event occurs that necessitates a meeting to decide what action the department or organisation should take.

 Your boss likes to have meetings for everything.

You must talk to colleagues who are working on the same project as you.

How do you know if meetings are causing you stress?

 You become bored, anxious and depressed at meetings.

 You feel as though meetings are wasting your time and you would rather be getting on with your work.

 When attending a meeting, you wish that it would soon end.

 You believe that whatever you say will make no difference – bosses are paid to make decisions.

 You know your colleagues at the meeting only speak to make themselves look good.

What can you do about it?

If you are chairing a meeting:

 Have an agenda and stick to it.

 Tell those who regularly arrive late (or don't attend) and do not have an acceptable excuse, that their behaviour has been noted.

 Keep to a strict timescale – meetings expand to fill the time available.

Ban mobile phones.

 If people have to stand at a meeting this can cut the meeting time.

 Make sure everyone knows what actions they will have to follow up.

If you are attending a meeting:

 Read the agenda.

 Ensure that you know the purpose of the meeting.

Ask yourself if you have to attend the meeting. Maybe you can skip the meeting and read the minutes.

Do any work you have to in advance of the meeting to make certain that you understand the topic under discussion.

9. How to get more pay

A recent survey found that poor pay and benefits are the main causes of stress at work for 12 per cent of UK employees. Do you get stressed when you think of how much you earn? Are you angry because your benefits are so low? Employees who are stressed by their finances often bring their concerns to the workplace. So it will 'pay' the employer to give their staff an adequate wage. In fact, it has been found that those employees who had higher levels of financial stress had lower levels of pay satisfaction. They were also more likely to waste their time at work and were absent from work more often. Whether employers are able to pay more or not, they can educate their employees to avoid running into financial difficulties – this can reduce absenteeism and increase productivity.

What can you do to get more pay?

Assuming you are not on a fixed pay scale – and therefore can't get a pay rise without a promotion – here are some actions you might take to try and secure a pay rise:

- Arrange to speak to your boss and indicate what the subject of the discussion will be. It will work to your advantage if you have just successfully finished a particular project that you can talk about.

- Make sure you know in advance what you want from the meeting and the arguments you will use to get what you want. State what you've achieved in the previous year; mention clients and other organisational managers that think you're doing a good job.

- Outline what you hope to achieve in the next year or so (but don't make promises you will be unable to keep).

- Remember your boss will know what your salary would be in other organisations and they may use this to argue that your pay is adequate – of course, you might use it to justify a pay rise.

You have to consider what your boss will think of your request. They will ask why you deserve a pay rise – give them a good reason. They will want to know how you have contributed to the bottom line of the organisation, how the department you are in runs better because of you, the new ideas you have brought to the company, and so on.

Your boss may be unable, for many reasons, to give you a pay rise. On the other hand, you might be able to obtain improved benefits, such as private medical cover or life insurance. So be ready to consider these alternatives.

There are also certain things you shouldn't do:

If your organisation already offers an annual pay rise or review, then you will need a very good reason for requesting an interim pay rise.

If your boss is in a bad mood, asking for a pay rise will not be helpful, so judge your timing as best you can.

Do not say that you will leave the organisation if you don't get a pay rise – you might just get your wish. If your boss turns down your request, find out from them what you need to do in future to be successful.

One psychological study suggests ten strategies that will help you to achieve a higher salary:

You should start the negotiations – don't leave it to your boss.

State the figure that you want before the other side does – they'll make it as low as possible.

Make your figure high – but not unreasonable.

Use humour – make a joke to relieve the tension.

Try to persuade and assert yourself.

Threaten to leave for a rival company, taking all your knowledge with you (although this is a high risk strategy).

Collaborate with your boss.

Opt for a win-lose solution (where you win), not a win-win situation. Research has shown that the former gets more money and the latter feels better. What do you want?

Do not attempt to compromise and accommodate the other side – you'll get less money.

Believe that you are worth the money.

10. How to cope with working in an open-plan office

If you've had to work in an open-plan office or 'hot-desked', or have been involved in 'hotelling', then you'll know what the company thinks the benefits are. They can reduce the expenses of their office overheads, occupancy costs, the space required by staff and the furniture needed. Open-plan offices can lead to bosses becoming more controlling because now they can see everyone and everything. Management use open-plan offices to improve communications – but this doesn't work. It's been shown that communications go on in designated meeting, conference or side rooms, and thus many groups in the office who would have been involved in the past are now excluded.

A recent report from researchers in Australia suggested that open-plan offices are more likely to create illness among the workforce. This is caused by the spreading of infections and the stress levels of staff are also increased. In this report, no less than 90 per cent of employees who worked in open-plan offices reported detrimental health and psychological effects. This was caused by poorer security, greater insecurity because of the lack of privacy, catching colds and low productivity. The spreading of viruses is particularly true where staff have to 'hot-desk' and use a keyboard that has been used by someone else. Staff also felt that in open-plan offices their colleagues could hear them on the phone and see what they were doing on their computer. The noise in the open-plan office was also a concern.

There is a lot of evidence showing that clerical workers are more satisfied with the traditional partitioned office. With these offices they can concentrate better on their job and talk to their colleagues in private. Older employees want more privacy. However, the organisation can alter an open-plan office to suit any changes that occur and this set-up costs less per head.

So your stress about working in an open-plan office may not be mistaken.

What can you do about it?

If your organisation has gone down the open-plan office route, then it will be difficult to change their strategy (although a drop in performance may persuade them otherwise). However, you can do some things to improve the situation you find yourself in.

 Personalise your space by putting up photographs, plant pots and objects that mean something to you.

 When colleagues interrupt you or make a noise, don't lose your temper. Wear earphones to show that you are working and don't want to be interrupted. In advance of this, you can have a chat with your co-workers to explain that you prefer to work quietly, so you'll be wearing earphones to help you concentrate.

 It's been found that employees in open-plan offices work longer hours. So make sure that you leave on time unless you really have to stay.

11. How to cope with a dull, boring, repetitive job

Is your job one that doesn't allow you to show your skills, knowledge and experience? Or that demands too little of your abilities and talents? It's not surprising that you get stressed. Lots of studies have shown employees with a job that doesn't challenge them are just as stressed as those with challenging work. Repetitive jobs result in an increase in boredom and monotony, lack of attention and many psychological problems. Assembly-line jobs tend to be repetitive, doing the same task over and over again, operating at a fixed speed, requiring minimal skills from the employee, and demanding little mental application. Much the same outcomes come from using a keyboard and computer for your work – these jobs are just as repetitive and restrictive. And with the use of computers comes electronic monitoring of staff –in itself a stressor – which, for example, affects those who work at the checkout of a supermarket or are employed by a call centre. Blue-collar roles have now seen a reduction in the negative effects of repetitive jobs, because many of them have now been automated – and now it is the white-collar tasks that are repetitive. These are tasks with a high work pace and low-decision latitude, and these very often result in a high risk of stress.

Repetitive jobs, such as working as a keyboard operator or an assembly-line worker, can result in psychological problems for the operative. These people can also suffer from repetitive strain injury (RSI). RSI can be caused by other repetitious situations at work, such as carrying heavy items, constantly holding your phone or sitting in the same position for long periods. The UK NHS claims that one worker in every 50 has reported an RSI condition.

What can you do about it?

In order to prevent RSI, the NHS suggests that if you work at a computer all day you should:

Make sure your seat, keyboard, mouse and screen are positioned so they cause the least amount of strain to your fingers, hands, wrists, neck and back.

Sit at your desk with a good posture. Adjust your chair so that your forearms are horizontal with the desk and your eyes are at the same height as the top of your computer screen.

Take short breaks from the work rather than a longer break at lunch.

If you're working at the checkout in a shop then you should:

Ask your boss to give you other tasks to do (such as stacking shelves or sweeping the floor) during the day.

Talk and be helpful to customers (of course, this assumes you have the time to do this).

Remember to get up and stretch from time to time. You might also try to stand up to do your work, have an ergonomically designed chair (supplied by your company) and ensure any equipment you have to use is positioned at the right height.

Remind yourself that you're only doing the job for the money and to get you out of the house.

Chapter 3

Your Role in the Organisation

12. Take control of your workload

Do you feel in control of your workload? The UK Health & Safety Executive (HSE) has said that employees should be given the opportunity to decide how they do their work and, where possible, have control over the pace of their work.

In order to take control of your workload, the first thing you must do is find out if you are an internally oriented (an internal) or an externally oriented (an external) individual. This is determined by your locus of control – the control that you feel you have over your work (and your life in general). If you are internally oriented you believe that your decisions and your behaviour affect what happens to you. On the other hand, if you're externally oriented you believe that luck or fate, rather than your actions, determines what happens to you.

Try this questionnaire about the control you think you have at work. Answer each question as quickly and honestly as you can.

Indicate the degree of your agreement or disagreement with each statement by giving each a score as follows:

5 = if you strongly agree with the statement

4 = if you agree with the statement

3 = if you feel so-so about the statement

2 = if you disagree with the statement

1 = if you strongly disagree with the statement.

1. The trouble with workers nowadays is they are subject to too many constraints and punishments.

2. Performance appraisals do not reflect how hard people work.

3. Lower-level staff cannot influence the way management behave.

4. Most of us are subject at work to influences we cannot control.

5. One's ability is not the main factor which determines promotion at work.

6. It is management who are responsible for the company performance, not ordinary employees.

7. The things that happen to people are controlled by luck or chance, rather than their own actions.

8. In organisations that are run by a few people, the average individual has little influence over decisions.

Add up your scores. The total will be between 8 and 40. If you scored less than 24 you tend to be an internal. If you scored more than 24 you are an external. If you scored exactly 24, then you're right in the middle – sometimes you're an internal, sometimes you're an external.

It was reported in 2006 that internal personalities tend to have favourable work outcomes, such as positive task and social experiences, and greater job motivation, and there is lots of evidence that control, even having the belief that you have control, is associated with myriad positive outcomes.

Lack of control is associated with various forms of ill health. In fact, low control at work was a predictor of suicide among Japanese male workers. This implies that redesigning jobs to give increased worker control might be a worthwhile strategy in preventing, or at least reducing, the risk of suicide. If you can self-pace your work and choose the tasks you undertake, evidence shows you'll have fewer symptoms of stress than those who don't have control at work. If, no matter what you do, you cannot affect the result, you may stop trying.

Incidentally, if you have much control over your job, and the job itself demands a lot from you, these are seen as the best kind of jobs from a stress and strain point of view. The worst kind of jobs, on the other hand, are jobs with low control and high demands. The University of Texas has reported that those who face few pressures and have little control over their jobs are up to 50 per cent more likely to die within ten years of quitting work compared with employees who have had major responsibilities at work. A famous study of civil servants in the UK shows that low job control can result in coronary heart disease among male and female civil servants. Heart disease can come from roles with low control, and if control is increased this will reduce the risk of coronary heart disease. Organisation policies that provide employees with a stronger say in decisions about their work or give them more variety in work tasks can contribute to better cardiovascular health.

How does it happen?

 Your organisation uses an assembly line.

 You are dependent on other people that you cannot control.

 The organisation in which you work imposes deadlines, tasks, etc. without consulting you.

How do you know when you are doing a job with low control?

 No matter what you do, you can't affect things at work.

 You have a repetitive, assembly-line type job and the assembly line goes at a constant, unchanging speed.

 You can't control the pace at which you have to work.

What can you do about it?

 Tell your manager that giving employees more control over their work has many benefits, among them better productivity, lower sickness absence and reduced staff turnover.

 Ask your colleagues not to send you any more work until you ask for it (if you can).

Make a list of all the tasks you want to do and plan when you're going to do them. At the beginning of each day, take time to plan what you're going to do before you go home. Do one thing at a time and at the end of the day spend a little time to think about what you've achieved that day. If you can, set a routine for the day.

> ### Congratulate yourself
>
> Measure your success at work through how you have progressed your workload, rather than how many tasks you have completed that day. Don't get disheartened if you haven't completed everything on your to-do list, but rather be proud of the level of work you have achieved.

13. What to do if your role in the organisation is ambiguous

When you're not sure what your work objectives are, you don't know what your colleagues expect you to do, and you are uncertain of your job's scope and responsibilities, then you're suffering from role ambiguity. Maybe this arises because your boss or supervisor hasn't told you exactly what you're supposed to be doing, where you fit into the organisation and what the rewards are for being successful. Or maybe you are working in an organisation where you've been promoted or transferred to another section, or your company has been taken over by or merged with another. You may have role ambiguity, where you don't know what your role is; or perhaps you have task ambiguity, where you have inadequate or confusing information about how to do your work; or you have what has been called socio-emotional ambiguity, where you don't know how the work that you do will affect you, your colleagues or your organisation.

Stress in the form of a depressed mood, lowered self-esteem, dissatisfaction with life in general, low motivation to work and the intention to leave the job are the outcomes of role ambiguity. In addition, role ambiguity has been shown to lead to tension and fatigue, high levels of anxiety, physical and psychological strain, and absenteeism. To manage it, you can, on the one hand, find out from your boss and colleagues what you're supposed to be doing, or, on the other hand, you can withdraw your support from some aspects of your work – this is not recommended if you want to keep your job.

Take this questionnaire to find out if you have any job ambiguity. Indicate the degree of your agreement or disagreement with each statement by giving each a score as follows:

1 = No

2 = A little

3 = An average amount

4 = Enough

5 = A lot

1. I have been given clear objectives for my job.

2. I know how much authority I have.

3. I work under vague instructions*.

4. I know exactly what I have to do in my job.

5. I understand what I have to do in my job to get a promotion or more money.

6. I have been given a clear explanation of what I have to do in my job.

7. I know how my job fits in with the work of my colleagues.

8. I am told when I'm doing a good job.

9. I know exactly what is expected of me.

10. I understand how my performance will be evaluated.

For the statement marked with a * your final score will be 6 minus the number you circled.

Add the ten scores.

 If you scored 10 to 20 you are working under job ambiguity.

 If you scored 21 to 39 you have some job ambiguity.

 If you scored 40 to 50 you are fairly certain about what you have to do.

How does it happen?

 You are in a new job and are unsure of the parameters of your role.

 You have been promoted and are struggling to adjust to the change in your job role.

 The training you have been given is inadequate for you to clearly define your role.

 You have little support from your boss and manager.

 Your organisation has been restructured.

How do you know if role ambiguity is causing you stress?

 You have job 'burnout'. Job burnout is defined by *Merriam-Webster's Collegiate Dictionary* as an 'exhaustion of physical or emotional strength or motivation, usually as a result of prolonged stress or frustration'. Job burnout is a particular kind of job stress – you are physically, emotionally or mentally exhausted (or all of these) combined with doubts about your competence and the value of your work.

 You are prevented from being productive. You may be bored or lethargic, you don't have a clear vision of what you're doing and why you're doing the job, or you take on too many tasks. You might need to get better or more sleep. You might also have to change your diet.

◯ You cope by being aggressive, you don't communicate properly with your workmates and you withdraw from some of your work.

◯ You ask yourself why you are doing the job.

What can you do about it?

◯ When you apply for or are asked to take on a job, ask for an adequate job description and induction. Job descriptions show the work you would be doing.

◯ Ask your boss to tell you what you have to do and define your job clearly. Be friendly when you speak to your boss – they may be unsure of all the tasks you have to carry out.

◯ Ensure that your organisation conducts an effective performance evaluation. You can use this (usually annual) process to find out what you are being measured on and you will know what your tasks for the coming period are.

◯ If you were given a job description, revisit it to ensure you are clear about what your role is, and do an audit on yourself to find out if you are fulfilling the job preview or you have fewer or extra tasks that are confusing your job role. If you are doing more than you were required to, make sure that you tell your boss. If you are doing less than you were expecting, you should point out to your boss those tasks that you were anticipating carrying out and are not doing, and find out why. If you want to do these tasks, you should tell your boss, but if you want to do something else, perhaps something that will get you noticed, then suggest these tasks to your boss.

14. How to overcome role conflict

Perhaps you are doing a job where you are torn by conflicting job demands, or you have to do things you don't want to, or things you don't feel are part of your job. Maybe people at work expect different kinds of behaviour from you or think your job has different functions than you do. If so, you may be suffering from role conflict. Role conflict may mean that you may suffer from one of these:

- Your boss or supervisor gives you conflicting demands (this is intra-sender role conflict).
- Your boss, manager or colleagues give you incompatible demands (this is inter-sender role conflict).
- You don't believe in the same things as your colleagues or the organisation (this is person-role conflict).
- You are doing a job where two (or more) of your roles are in conflict (this is inter-role conflict).
- You are expected to behave in a way that is too complicated or difficult, or you are required to show too many behaviours in the time available (this is an example of role overload).

As a result, the employee who encounters role conflict has reduced job satisfaction, an increase in anxiety and doesn't communicate with those people who are causing the role conflict. Research indicates that role conflict is most associated with gastrointestinal problems.

An example of role conflict is that of the nurse's role. Nurses are expected to carry out certain duties as laid down by their supervisor or manager. They are also expected to meet the requirements of their colleagues, who could be other nurses, hospital staff, etc. At the same time, the nurse has to meet the expectations of their professional association or college/university. The nurse has also to meet their own requirements and be able to match up to their own image of themselves. When each of these elements are in sync there are no problems for the nurse. But often, these sets of expectations are in conflict and this negatively affects the nurse's motivation, job satisfaction and productivity, and leads them to feel stressed.

Managers, too, can be affected by role conflict. During the global financial crisis of the 2010s, many organisations have had to reduce their costs. Managers may be suffering from the two conflicting goals of maintaining the job security of staff and at the same time keeping staff costs to a minimum. The same constraints and pressures experienced by nurses – as described above – will be felt by such individuals.

Working women, in particular, suffer from role conflict. Typically, they do the majority of household chores, and are mainly responsible for child rearing and other family activities, while juggling full-time jobs. Many women report the conflict of the job interfering with their role in keeping the family on an even keel. Research indicates that women are more affected than men by the intrusion of work into their homes. Women feel more guilt and psychological distress when they are contacted at home by bosses, colleagues or clients. Research has also shown that role conflict at work reduces men's marital satisfaction – that is, their satisfaction with the work they do at home with children, spouses, housekeeping, etc.

How does it happen?

The organisation has not thought through what it is asking you to do.

Your role in the organisation has grown.

The people who report to you are in some way incompetent.

How do you know if role conflict is causing you stress?

○ The work that you are doing is too difficult because you are being pulled in different directions by different people.

○ The responsibilities you have been given are incompatible with each other.

○ Different people have different expectations of you. For example, if you are a teacher one person expects you to have a high pass rate in a topic, while another person expects you to maintain a high level of quality. Sometimes the two outcomes are incompatible.

○ Your beliefs and values are different from those of the organisation.

What can you do about it?

○ Set goals for your role at work. One way to do this is to use SMART work objectives. SMART work objectives are Specific, Measurable, Achievable, Realistic, Timely. Show your objectives to your boss. This is what you propose to achieve and it will help you to clarify your role.

○ Suggest to your boss that an away-day for staff would be useful to discuss and reduce the sources of role conflict. Away-days can be used to share ideas and improve teamwork, and they needn't cost much.

○ Suggest to your boss that an increase in worker participation in decision-making can reduce role conflict. This can be done by having staff sharing in the company's success (by owning shares and participating in profits), using suggestion schemes and quality circles, etc. As an employee, you will not be able to install these items, but you can gain 'brownie points' by pointing out these to your manager.

15. What to do if people disapprove of your role

Maybe you are apprehensive about telling people what you do for a living. Maybe you work for an organisation that has a very bad reputation. Even though you like your job, no one else does. Sound familiar? No wonder you get stressed. A recent survey held in the USA showed the most admired job was that of a firefighter (not surprising after 11 September 2001), followed by doctors, nurses, scientists and military officers. The least admired were lawyers, journalists and union leaders. That, of course, is the USA. In the UK, the most admired people were those in those in the armed forces, followed by rescue volunteers, nurses, veterinarians, teachers, ambulance drivers, firefighters, care assistants, rugby players and police officers. These are admired jobs, but what about the most hated professions? The most hated profession in the UK was that of the traffic warden, followed by bouncers, estate agents, motorcycle couriers, bus drivers, footballers, people in telesales, those who work in public relations, politicians and anyone who takes part in reality TV shows. And if you're a banker you'll be used to getting a lot of abuse.

What can you do?

Well, you could remind yourself that it's the other person's problem if they do not like your job. Or you could just grin and bear it. You could remind yourself of why you embarked upon your job and think about the things that you like about it. Try to rationalise what it is about your job that others dislike and find a way of justifying your decision to work in that role. You could get some support from your fellow employees, those who work in the same organisation as you or do similar work. If you end up with too much stress to bear, you could always try to leave for another job.

For instance, those of you who work in an IT department come in for a lot of abuse. However, the IT department has to balance its budget and time. Once people understand this they should appreciate them a little more. So if you work in an IT department, tell employees in other departments what your constraints are. The same solution applies to jobs that others disapprove of. Ensure they know the benefits to both them and to the organisation of the work you are doing, as well as the constraints you have to work under.

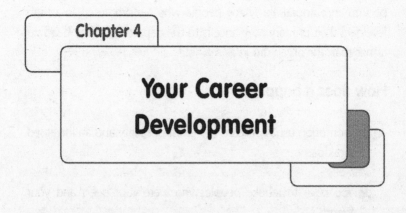

Chapter 4

Your Career Development

16. How to deal with the strain of a promotion

Have you been promoted and find this is causing you more stress than usual? Researchers at the University of Warwick have found that on average promotion exerts 10 per cent more mental strain and allows up to 20 per cent less time to visit the doctor. It is assumed that an improvement to a person's job status will directly result in better health due to an increased sense of control over life and of self-worth – but researchers found no evidence of improved physical health after a promotion. They did find, however, that there was an increase of mental strain. Being promoted is more challenging than most other major life events, including divorce or the death of a loved one, according to researchers studying managers and executives at a consulting firm. In addition, companies tend to under-prepare their employees to handle the increased responsibilities of promotion. Anything that puts high demands on you or forces you to adjust your work or life can be stressful. It has been reported that 40 per cent of first-time managers come to grief within 18 months of their promotion: they get sacked, are forced to resign or get bad performance appraisals. Many people who are promoted to a high level feel their primary allegiance is to the department they head up rather than the organisation as a whole.

How does it happen?

 Promotion usually means more responsibility and an increased workload.

 You have to rebuke people who were your peers and your friends.

 You are worried you'll make a mess of the work you now have to do.

 You have had a promotion but have no sense of more control.

 You worry that you don't have all the answers.

How do you know a promotion is causing you stress?

 You spend more of your day dealing with internal politics and planning, and have less time to do the actual work.

 There is more ambiguity and uncertainty surrounding your work.

You have to rely on other people in order to get things done.

Your partner at home has to do much more without you.

You have less free time.

The new role is not what you thought it would be.

What can you do about it?

Ask your boss what is expected from your role (make sure your boss is focused on your development).

Get support for your new position. You can do this in a number of ways. Find a mentor within the organisation, someone who will help you grow and develop in your new role. Perhaps this could be a person who has a job at the same level as you and is carrying out a similar role, so you can see how they deal with the stresses and strains. Or find a role model within the organisation. A role model is someone who inspires you and whose behaviour you want to emulate. Find someone in the organisation (or outside if there is no one suitable) whose values are similar to yours, whose choices you respect, who does the things you'd like to do, who treats people the way you want to be treated, and who walks and talks as you'd like to. You could also have a meeting with your new team: tell them what you expect from them, and what they can expect from you and your plans for the future. You could follow this up by meeting with each member of your team individually. You could also talk the issue through with your friends, family and your boss. Use any programme that your organisation offers to those who have been newly promoted.

17. How to cope with job insecurity

Fears over job security are felt worldwide. An investigation into the job security of employees in 17 countries in Europe found that in ten years it had dropped from 70 per cent to 48 per cent in the UK, and similar reductions had occurred in Germany, France, the Netherlands, Belgium and Italy, among others. For many people, job insecurity has replaced guaranteed employment.

If you anticipate losing your job, the effects on your health are just as bad as if you actually lost the job. Research has shown that job insecurity results in more mental health problems, such as depression and anxiety; higher rates of absenteeism; an increase in the use of health care services; more back pain; and, if you're a parent, concerns about your job can affect your children. If you're certain you will lose your job this causes less stress and burnout, rather than continual worry that you might lose your job. So knowing you're going to get the sack is better for you than continual doubt. A major study has shown that employees who are afraid of losing their jobs go into what has been called an 'anticipatory phase', and employees who have been sacked or made redundant are in a 'termination phase'. In the latter, they can tackle the consequences and stop worrying about what might happen.

Of course, redundancy affects income, but it also negatively alters the way people regard themselves. The loss of job is associated with ulcers, alopecia, colitis and muscular complaints, among other things. (And don't forget even those who survive the cutbacks and retain their jobs may suffer from psychological problems – they ask themselves why they survived and whether they'll be next.)

How does it happen?

 Your organisation is downsizing, merging or going out of business.

 Your organisation is restructuring.

 Your organisation is outsourcing tasks.

 You are a 'casual' employee – for instance, doing temporary or part-time work.

 Older workers are the first to go – they are seen as expensive and more difficult to train.

How do you know if job insecurity is causing you stress?

 You feel anxious about your job security.

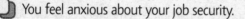 You are a victim of 'presenteeism', which means you spend more time at work than is required and even go to work when you are unwell. You might come to work even though you're ill because you're worried about losing your job if you're absent, you need the money, or you are devoted to the job and your workmates.

 You are experiencing problems at work, such as poor interpersonal relationships. There may be a major discrepancy between how you would like to be treated and how you are actually treated, or workplace communications need improving.

There is competition for the limited number of roles that will remain after your department or company cuts jobs in its workforce.

There is more resistance to change among employees, reduced morale, etc.

If you lose your job or are concerned about losing your job, what can you do about it?

It is helpful to create a security net for yourself to cushion you from the pressures of alienation. For example, keep up with friends with whom you can chew over your problems – remember the old adage, a problem shared is a problem halved, and this will stand you in good stead.

If you can't change your job (not easy when the economy is problematic), consider other forms of employment – work for yourself, become a part-time, temporary or casual worker. Remember these roles may fall under different employment laws, and the salary you obtain may not be the same as you have become used to.

Seek support from colleagues if you are concerned you may be made redundant.

You might consider taking on work that is completely different from what you are used to.

Keep your skills relevant and up to date – and not just your technical skills, but also communication and leadership. You can do this by reading relevant articles or books, or by signing up for courses specifically designed to give you what you need. Doing this may help you to stick to a job even though you are worried about losing it.

It is always useful to keep your CV up to date, ready for any eventuality.

Make a list of all your options, should you be unfortunate enough to lose your job. A list will allow you to think more clearly about how you can deal with eventualities rather than leave all of your worries swimming around in your head. This will help you to relax, be able to sleep better and, as a result, reduce your stress levels.

A problem shared

Friends don't only provide a shoulder to lean on but also a comforting, familiar environment to relieve you from the uncertainty of your work life. Spend time with good friends and enjoy some of your favourite activities together. Talk through your problems at work but ensure that it isn't the only topic of conversation and enjoy the good company.

18. How to cope with being over-promoted – or under-promoted

You know what it's like: you didn't get the promotion you deserved and, what is even worse, it went to a less competent colleague. On the other hand, you've been given a promotion and find that you just can't do the job: it's beyond your capabilities. When you are promoted too quickly and find yourself doing a job for which you are not qualified, you may feel that ultimately you might lose that job. In both cases you are totally stressed. Under-promotion, the feeling of being unduly delayed in your career progress, is a common source of stress. Almost every writer on stress at work cites over-promotion and under-promotion as major stressors, and they have both been shown to result in mental illness. Over-promotion (when you have responsibilities beyond your capabilities, and which can be exacerbated by lack of further promotion prospects), and under-promotion (when you have not been given responsibilities commensurate with your actual or self-perceived abilities) can result in psychological issues such as anxiety, depression and psychosomatic symptoms. Psychosomatic means mind (psyche) and body (soma). Some physical diseases are thought to be caused or aggravated by stress and anxiety, for example eczema, high blood pressure, psoriasis and heart disease.

Women in particular suffer from under-promotion and, especially, from over-promotion. Women tend not to get promoted if they are in competition with men. In addition, there are many more women than men suffering from 'imposter syndrome' – when they are holding down a job they feel under-qualified for. Research has estimated that two out of five successful people believe they are 'frauds', even though they have been promoted due to their superior performance. This is quite common among promoted personnel and it has been found that as many as 70 per cent of successful people reported feeling like fakes at one time or another. Women, it was found, may question their worth more than men.

How does it happen?

- In recent years, many organisations have downsized and removed whole layers of staff (delayered). There are now fewer of the traditional promoted posts available.

- You are stuck in a job with no prospects of promotion.

What can you do?

- Take any lateral move the organisation offers you.

- Keep learning new techniques (see previous examples of how this can be achieved).

- Although it applies to very few people, if you are over 50 years old and can't stand the situation you are in any more, then consider taking early retirement and lift your pension (if you have one).

- Arrange a meeting with your boss to discuss your job role, any training that may be available or the possibility of being mentored by an appropriate person. The Oxford School of Coaching & Mentoring says: 'Mentoring is to support and encourage people to manage their own learning in order that they may maximise their potential, develop their skills, improve their performance and become the person they want to be.'

Speak to your boss and find out what you could have done differently in order to get a promotion, and ask how you can ensure you won't miss out in the future.

Ask yourself why you haven't been promoted. It might be that although you are very competent you are not the kind of person who will develop others – which is what is expected of managers and team leaders. Maybe you are poor at making decisions when presented with many alternatives, and are not known for taking risks or responsibility. Or perhaps you tend to agree with everyone and prefer to avoid confrontation, even though situations arise which require tough feedback. By determining your weaknesses you can take action on them to improve your chances of future promotion.

19. How to overcome any lack of training

If you've not been given adequate training, it's likely you won't be able to do the job well and a lack of training can cause stress. It is generally reported that UK managers receive little or no training on how to be a manager and only get formal training from their employer when they specifically request it. This is a very serious issue among 25 to 34 year olds who aspire to be managers. They need the training.

If you feel that training will improve your performance, you have the right to ask your employer for 'time to train', as long as the training will lead to a qualification or will help you to develop the skills relevant to your job, workplace or business. The most important requirement is that the training you ask for will lead to better business performance and improve your effectiveness at work.

The training can be held at your workplace (even if you work at home), it can be obtained via the Internet, you can go to your local college or a private organisation, your employer can provide the training, or it can be any combination of these.

The UK law about training states that if you work for an organisation with 250 or more employees you have the right to request time for study or training. But you must have worked for your employer continuously for at least 26 weeks. There are some exceptions, however, including agency workers and members of the armed forces. Make sure you know where you stand. Employers must consider your request – they can turn it down but only if they have a good business reason for doing so.

If you work in smaller organisation the rules are different. You'll have to arrange your own training, which you can do by taking a course through the Open University, by reading, going to your local college or by looking at items on the Internet. Of course, you can ask your boss to give you (and your colleagues) the training and explain how this will help the organisation.

Hopefully your employer currently provides as much training as you need. However, there are some jobs that need specific training, especially to deal with the stress associated with the role, for example, doctors, nurses, firefighters, police, aircraft crew, etc.

How does it happen?

◯ Your organisation does not offer training.

◯ Your organisation expects you to do your own training.

You've been promoted to a post or asked to do work of which you don't have any experience or knowledge.

Your organisation has a high turnover of staff and so doesn't believe training staff is worthwhile.

What can you do?

If you can, find a mentor within the organisation – someone who will give you the benefit of their own experience.

Tell your boss you need some training to help you to do your job more efficiently, and explain how such training would bring benefits to the department and the organisation. Make a list of the areas of your job in which you feel you need training and work out what the positive impact such training would provide. Once you have this information you can approach your boss with suggestions. If your boss can clearly see how such training will benefit the organisation they are far more likely to arrange it for you.

Train yourself by finding a course. The first thing to do is to determine what training you need. You can then find out if there is a suitable course in a local college. You could also read a book on the topic or find information on the Internet.

20. How to cope with giving a presentation

It's quite normal to be nervous when you have to give a presentation at work, but you can make the nerves work for you. In fact, if you don't feel some nervousness you won't do a good job. The best speakers, opera singers and actors, among others, rely on a certain amount of nervousness (which produces adrenaline) to do their job well.

How does it happen?

 You have made a presentation before and it wasn't very good.

You have not prepared for the presentation.

You have not rehearsed the presentation.

You have not prepared answers to the questions you are likely to be asked.

You lack confidence and are unaccustomed to speaking in front of others.

What causes it?

 You are concerned you will be compared with your colleagues.

There will be negative outcomes for you if you do not do well.

You are concerned about how your colleagues will react to your presentation.

Your manager and senior personnel will be in the audience at your presentation.

What can you do about it?

There are numerous aids to help you make competent presentations. Here are some strategies that you should follow:

 First, dress smartly, because this shows your audience that you care about them and your clothes will not distract from the points you are making.

 Smile and appear confident and enthusiastic (even if you're not).

Say 'hello' to your audience. Ask people at the back if they can hear you and can see everything you are showing on the screen.

Speak at a pace that will allow your audience to take in what you are saying. If you talk quickly your voice tends to raise its pitch.

 Don't worry about pauses – it's natural to have breaks.

Maintain eye contact with your audience. A good speaker often appears to be looking at you directly.

If you can introduce some laughter and jokes (just a few) into your presentation, do so.

Make sure you are confident about the topic of your presentation and that you know what you're talking about.

Stick to the time you have been allocated for the presentation.

Don't forget to practise your talk in advance, even if it seems an unimportant topic. Articulating your speech out loud in front of a mirror before a presentation is well worth doing, as you can get an idea of how you are going to come across to your audience. Over time, you'll get better at giving presentations.

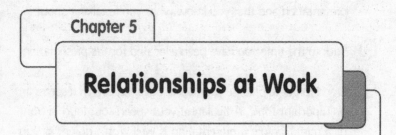

Chapter 5

Relationships at Work

21. How to deal with your emotions at work

If you've ever had a job working in retail, in a restaurant dealing with customers, in a bank, or as a nurse, or suchlike, you will know it is important to behave in a friendly manner and adopt a smiling face. Undoubtedly, there will have been some occasions when smiling went against the grain but you kept up appearances nonetheless. This is emotional labour, which is the way an employee expresses the emotions required by the organisation when dealing with other people (who could be customers or colleagues) at work.

The idea of emotional labour began with a study of service workers such as flight attendants (they are expected always to be cheerful), funeral directors (whom we always expect to be mournful) and doctors (whom we expect to be emotionally neutral). In fact, almost every job now has an element of emotional labour. In the UK, we have moved from a manufacturing to a service economy, and in jobs which involve call centres, social care, customer service, welfare benefits, etc., you are expected to treat customers and colleagues in a friendly manner, even if you don't like them! This means there is sometimes a disparity between how you'd like to behave and how the organisation requires you to behave. This disparity is called emotional dissonance and can result in emotional exhaustion and burnout (burnout is an extreme state of psychological strain and depletion of energy resources) in the employee. It can lead to job dissatisfaction, absenteeism and higher staff turnover.

As an example of emotional labour, let's look at a study of customer service representatives (CSRs) in a call centre, carried out by the Centre for Organisation & Innovation at the University of Sheffield. In relation to emotional labour, the CSRs expressed more positive emotions than they actually felt. Concerning emotional dissonance, the CSRs expressed more positive emotions than they felt on about 50 per cent of occasions, but expressed more negative feelings than they felt on about 20 per cent of occasions. CSRs hid negative feelings half the time but also suppressed positive feelings about a fifth of the time. They also felt and displayed more positive emotions when customers and co-workers were more pleasant, the workload was lower and it was earlier in the day. The CSRs expressed more negative emotions when customers were more unpleasant.

How does it happen?

Your organisation requires you to be friendly to customers, clients and colleagues.

Your organisation has decided to focus greater attention on customers and clients.

You must manage the emotions you display towards customers, suppressing some and expressing others, be they genuine or contrived.

How do you know when you are engaged in emotional labour?

○ You show emotions you don't really feel.

○ You hide emotions you really do feel.

○ You create an appropriate emotion for the situation.

○ You are paid, in part, to manage and control your emotions.

What can you do about it?

○ Learn to separate the emotions you feel from the emotions you show, even though this may be stressful. You can do this if you learn to relax and learn about body language, because body language can give out signals you might not want it to. You should also find something positive about the situation you are in. Remember, practice makes perfect, so after a while you will be able to show the emotions you want to.

○ If you are a manager or employer, you should consider using buffering. Buffering consists of assigning front-end personnel to manage the emotional demands and needs of customers. When customers reach back-end workers after they've seen the front-end staff, both the customer and the back-end worker can concentrate on the business at hand. If you're an employee, you might approach your boss and ask them to consider using buffering – buffering will help you and the business.

◯ Your organisation can teach 'display' rules – approved norms or standards that you learn through observation, instruction, feedback and reinforcement. You are taught how to act and may even be given scripts to use when dealing directly with clients.

◯ Organisations can invest in emotional health services. If your organisation uses an EAP (Employee Assistance Programme) this may offer an emotional health service that provides information and emotional support on a range of issues. Through this, employees can learn how to control their emotions. Perhaps a local organisation offers an emotional health service – for instance, members of the public can use the emotional health service of the Sandyford Initiative located in Glasgow. You can find a directory of organisations, helplines and drop-in centres at www.bbc.co.uk/health/support/mental_health_emotional_usefulcontacts_index.shtml.

◯ You can ask your boss to bring emotional labour into the performance evaluation process. The evaluation process should indicate that you have displayed the right amount of emotional labour.

22. How to obtain interpersonal support at work

Do you get lots of support at work from your colleagues? Do they help you with your work? Do they provide you with emotional support? Do they tell you how well (or badly) you're doing? Perhaps

Schedule yourself in

Set aside some of your personal time to spend by yourself. Solitude can provide freedom from emotional pressures and allow you to express your feelings exactly as you wish. Use this time to do something you enjoy – it could be anything from listening to a piece of music you particularly connect to, to watching a favourite film or taking a long walk.

they don't. A study of nurses showed that respect, empathy and genuineness from their colleagues were important ingredients in helping relationships. In an examination of civil servants, work absenteeism was associated with a less supportive atmosphere. Furthermore, in the latter examination it was found psychosomatic symptoms were associated with lack of support at work. It has also been shown that if you get social support at work you will have less depression, job dissatisfaction, dissatisfaction with life in general and fewer somatic complaints.

Perhaps your section or department has been merged with another (or your organisation has merged with another company). You might feel that the new boss doesn't know you and does not appreciate your work. Perhaps you feel there is overt discrimination because your new supervisor comes from the other unit or department.

Social support can be found both at work from your bosses, supervisors and colleagues, and from your family and friends. Each of these relationships has been examined and results show that having a considerate boss or supervisor results in less stress for the employee.

There are different types of support you may need at work. It has been suggested these are emotional support, financial support, psychological support, political support, managerial support, organisational support and spiritual support. Try writing the names of people who give you support of each of these types. That will give you an idea of the support you get at work and any areas that are lacking. You can then try to seek out any support you need.

Attempt this questionnaire about the support you have at work. Answer each question as quickly and honestly as you can, giving each a score as follows.

5 = if you strongly agree with the statement

4 = if you agree with the statement

3 = if you are so-so about the statement

2 = if you disagree with the statement

1 = if you strongly disagree with the statement

1. There is a person around at work when you need.
2. Your family tries to help you with your work problems.
3. Your friends try to help you with your work problems.
4. You can depend on your colleagues to help you at work.
5. You can depend on your boss to help you at work.
6. In general you can trust the people you work with.
7. You can talk to your colleagues about your problems.
8. You can talk to your boss about your problems.

There is no right or wrong score; your answers will give you something to consider. If you have a high score, clearly you have a good deal of support; a lower score indicates you would benefit from more support.

How does it happen?

 People in the organisation are only concerned with their own work.

 Other people see you as unhelpful.

 Your colleagues have poor interpersonal skills.

How do you know you have poor interpersonal support at work?

 You have a sense of isolation at work.

 You cannot call on anyone for help at work.

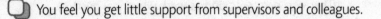 You feel you get little support from supervisors and colleagues.

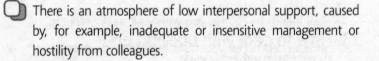 There is an atmosphere of low interpersonal support, caused by, for example, inadequate or insensitive management or hostility from colleagues.

What can you do about it?

Suggest to your boss ways in which your colleagues could form closer or stronger relationships. For example, have a company picnic where you can get to know your colleagues and vice versa.

Suggest to your employer that a coffee room be set up where you can meet and talk to your colleagues.

Ask your boss if you and your colleagues can have some training to improve interpersonal relationships. It'll improve the performance of the group (and your own career and job success).

Become a good listener. If people come to you with their problems, you will in turn get more support from them.

If you are a carer outside work, colleagues can be very supportive. Discuss this with them – you may find they also have caring responsibilities and your employer may help you to set up a support group.

You could think about setting up an after-hours club for work colleagues, for example, a book club, pub quiz team, football or rounders team, to offer less confident staff members an opportunity to meet and talk to others in an informal setting.

23. How to deal with bullying and harassment at work

We take bullying and harassment at work to be the same thing. A recent investigation into the stress effects of bullying on employees, and the stress effects of bullying on those who witness it at work, came up with some very interesting results. Five per cent of women and 5 per cent of men reported being bullied at work, with 9 per cent of the women and 11 per cent of the men having witnessed bullying at work. Those who were bullied at work showed they had lower social support from their fellow workers and supervisors, and they also reported more symptoms of somatic problems, more depression, anxiety and more emotional problems. Those who witnessed bullying reported they had more anxiety and obtained lower support from their supervisor.

In addition, the subject of post-traumatic stress disorder (PTSD) has been examined from the point of view of bullied employees. Several studies have suggested that victims of bullying may suffer from PTSD. What does PTSD feel like? The UK Royal College of Psychiatrists says that PTSD can result in the employee feeling grief-stricken, depressed, anxious, guilty and angry. They can suffer flashbacks and nightmares of the occasions of bullying; they avoid places and people that remind them of the event(s); they try not to talk about it by becoming emotionally numb – victims communicate less with other people who, in turn, find it hard to live or work with them, and the bullied person is continually on guard. Other psychosomatic symptoms can arise, too. The bullied person can have aches and pains, suffer diarrhoea and headaches, drink too much alcohol and feel depressed. One study reported that 76 per cent of employees who had been bullied showed symptoms of PTSD, with nearly 62 per cent indicating a moderate to severe level of impairment, and 73.6 per cent indicating a moderate or severe impairment. It is concluded that being bullied can result in increased negative views, not only on the bullied employee but on other people and the world in general. It has also been suggested that the climate of the organisation can determine whether bullying results in PTSD. This occurs when the organisation does not treat the bullied person and bullying is accepted by the organisation.

When you feel you are being bullied at work, you might want to think about why people, including your boss, might be bullies. Examples of underlying reasons are:

 The organisation has a culture of bullying.

 They have low self-esteem and don't regard themselves as having much worth.

They don't feel they have sufficient power over other people in the organisation.

They may be bullied themselves at work or at home.

They have an aggressive personality (for instance, it was found that bosses who weren't organised and were not mindful of details were always anxious or were themselves suffering from stress).

They don't consider the effect their bullying has on other people.

If you understand the reasons why people bully you may be able to do something about it. But maybe you don't have time to deal with your boss's problems, you just want the bullying to stop.

How does it happen?

 You are made fun of in front of your colleagues.

You are lied about behind your back.

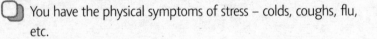 You feel as if you're always on your guard.

There are poor relationships at work.

The culture at work encourages bullying.

There is an over-competitive environment at work.

Colleagues are afraid of being made redundant.

A rigid style of management exists within the organisation.

How do you know if concern about bullying is causing you stress?

You suffer from anxiety, sleeplessness and fatigue.

 You have the physical symptoms of stress – colds, coughs, flu, etc.

You show the psychological symptoms of stress, such as panic attacks and depression.

 You worry about meeting the bully.

Your personality changes – your self-confidence and self-esteem are lowered.

What can you do about it?

Tell the bully their behaviour is not acceptable and ask them to stop. Here is how you might do this.

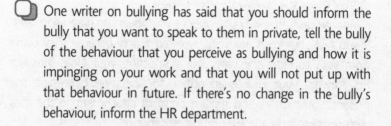

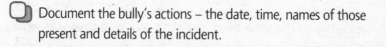Document the bully's actions – the date, time, names of those present and details of the incident.

You must not play the bully's game – keep your temper and do not react .

One writer on bullying has said that you should inform the bully that you want to speak to them in private, tell the bully of the behaviour that you perceive as bullying and how it is impinging on your work and that you will not put up with that behaviour in future. If there's no change in the bully's behaviour, inform the HR department.

Ask a supervisor or union member to be with you when you approach the bully.

If you maintain a record of the bully's actions you can use this should you need to take further action.

24. What to do if your ideas are always rejected

Maybe your boss, supervisor or colleagues are causing you problems. Everything you say they tend to argue with or they find faults with your suggestions. Try as you might, you cannot get them to understand your ideas. In your opinion they're simply idiots for not agreeing to your suggestions.

Perhaps your boss or manager has been promoted beyond their ability – this is quite common. A person does well at their work and so is promoted to head up a department. They receive no management training so you are left with a boss who cannot understand your suggestions. The same thing applies to your colleagues – especially if you are a member of a voluntary committee, perhaps a charity. Your colleagues are nice people, they are willing to give up their time, often for free, but they are just incapable of understanding your suggestions. They completely ignore your advice, but you can't change them so don't waste your energy.

In some cases, the way you present your ideas can have an impact. If you feel your ideas are being rejected simply because they come from you, consider the way you are putting your ideas forward. Put forward your idea as an option for the project, keeping the presentation neutral, and replace personal attachment to the idea with practical facts and supporting evidence.

Perhaps your boss isn't that bad at all – your personalities just clash. Your boss may be an extravert, while you are an introvert, and you cannot work out how to approach them. Your boss cannot appreciate your behaviour and at the same time you find their style unpleasant.

How does it happen?

 Your boss, supervisor or manager is out of their depth. They should not have been given the job in the first place.

 You join an organisation or are a member of a group that does not understand what you are trying to explain to them.

 You have not explained your point very well.

How do you know if you can't get your ideas accepted?

Bosses and colleagues never agree with your well-presented case.

People always find a reason for not doing what you suggest.

Whatever you suggest is laughed at or you're told it would never work.

Your colleagues and boss are stuck in the past and do not listen to new ideas.

What can you do about it?

Improve your communication skills. The aim of superior communication skills is mutual understanding and finding a solution that pleases both parties – not 'winning' the argument or 'being right'. So aim for a win-win outcome where both parties can get something out of the situation. Be respectful of the other person(s), even though you don't like their arguments or actions. Listen to other people and try to see their point of view. If you or your argument are criticised, listen to the other person and try to see their point of view.

Accept the weaknesses of your colleagues, bosses, etc. This will make working with them more enjoyable and less stressful. If you want, you can use your colleagues' weaknesses to your own advantage at work. But always remember that none of us are perfect.

Tell your boss's manager – but remember that your boss was selected by the organisation. You might be regarded as the problem.

Learn as much as you can from a weak boss or poor colleagues. Ask yourself why they are weak and what is missing from their behaviour. You can then compensate by fixing the weakness yourself, and tell yourself when you are in a more senior position you won't make the same mistakes.

Show others you are able to work with people you disagree with or don't find it easy to work with.

Value yourself

Rejection can affect your self-esteem in any circumstances. Spend time reminding yourself of your good qualities and the positive attributes you bring to the team.

25. How to cope with sacking people

When you have to sack someone or make them redundant, it can be a very stressful task. If you're a manager, at some point in your career you'll probably have to dismiss an employee. It can be difficult and emotional for both parties. If you have to sack an employee on the grounds of a misdemeanour, such as theft or incompetence, then it's pretty straightforward. It's more difficult if your organisation is simply cutting back. The question most managers ask is whether there is a kind way to let someone go? The general answer is no.

Imagine the situation: a member of a team has been caught stealing and you have to sack them. The way you might handle this is to meet the offender in a quiet room and ask if they would like to resign (as this might help them to obtain a job in future). If they don't want to resign then you'll have to sack them.

Follow the regulations. Make sure you know all the facts – where and when the offence took place, etc. Have a colleague with you (usually a member of the HR department) and the employee should be allowed to bring a friend, professional adviser or a union representative.

In advance, you should make sure all staff know what would lead to instant dismissal – insubordination, excessive absence, stealing, etc. In a medium-sized organisation the HR department should do this; in a smaller organisation the director or equivalent should inform staff of the company regulations. If an employee has not been doing their job, you should explain the performance is not satisfactory, state what the employee has to do if they want to continue to be employed and if they do not improve the next action will be termination of employment. Keep a signed (by you and by the employee) record of what has been discussed – you may need this if the employee takes action against the organisation. If you have to sack an employee, inform the individual why you are meeting them and get the event over with as quickly as possible. There may be repercussions from the other person – be ready for this – and you might feel unhappy about having to sack someone.

Make sure you know the legal position – you may need to take advice on this. Also, you should remember the effect of the sacking on other employees. If the sacking is justified, as it should be, then other employees will accept it as correct. If the sacking is unjustified, then not only may you have to face legal action, but other employees will be affected and may fear and dislike you – and you'll lose credibility with them.

Unless the dismissed person has committed a dreadful misdemeanour, do the sacking as ethically as you can and leave the dismissed person with some pride.

You'll find it gets easier to dismiss people over time.

How does it happen?

An employee has to be dismissed because they are redundant, or have been found guilty of committing a misdemeanour that warrants their dismissal.

How do you know if you have to dismiss an employee?

An employee has been made redundant, is not able to do the work required or has been found guilty of committing a misdemeanour.

What can you do about it?

Understand the legal requirements for dismissing an employee and ensure you understand your organisation's rules for employee dismissal. It is never going to be easy to sack someone and it will not leave you with a good feeling, but you need to draw on your professionalism in these instances. Keep in mind the task is not 'personal' and it is happening for a valid reason. Try to avoid making the dismissal an emotional event.

26. How to get on with your colleagues

Is it difficult for you to get along with any of your colleagues? Do you dread having to talk to one of your workmates? At work there is always the chance one of your fellow workers might be disagreeable and easy to upset. Maybe one of your co-workers is making you so stressed that you avoid approaching them, but if you have to talk to them you anticipate that with horror. You can choose your friends but, like your relatives, you can't choose your colleagues. The odds are there will be some people you just can't get on with.

What can you do about it?

It will be difficult, but here are some actions you can take. Remember that some people are incapable of being pleasant, so in these cases you'll just have to keep your contact with them down to a minimum.

- Respect your colleagues and try not to offend them in any way. Be mindful of their opinions.

- Avoid certain topics. Inflammatory areas include sport, religion, politics, your health, your hopes and plans for your career, your home life and your sex life.

- If you are starting a new job, try to be friendly to your colleagues, get to know and understand them, and try to accept any advice that they give you (and thank them for it).

- Do not gossip about your colleagues, especially if you work with a vicious gossip. The office grapevine is something quite different and you should listen to what comes through this – but take everything you hear with a pinch of salt and be sceptical.

Take care when you're sending an email or using your mobile phone. Don't say something you'll regret later and keep the ringtone volume low on your phone.

If you're told something in confidence, keep it to yourself – don't be a gossip.

Be careful what you say and do at the office party – don't get drunk.

Be polite to everyone and offer to help them if you can. You may meet them again or need them when you're on the way up – or down.

Respect your colleagues' opinions. You also show your reaction to these opinions by your facial expressions and body language, so don't forget about these. Their opinions may be more valid than yours.

Don't show your colleagues that you will support your boss no matter what.

Be tolerant. You are certain to clash with other people at some time. Make allowances for this and try not to become overly upset by such incidents.

If you just cannot get on with a colleague, and perhaps you've had an argument with them, then what can you do? You'll have to tell your boss your relationship with a colleague at work is beginning to affect your work. Hopefully they can resolve the problem. The best thing you can do is talk to your colleague; communication is the key.

> ### Have a laugh
>
> If you simply don't get on with a colleague, it can be easy to translate their every action into a deliberate attempt to annoy you. You may well have to work with them on a long-term basis so tackling the underlying stress can be helpful. Laughing regularly has been shown to increase levels of serotonin – the hormone that makes you happy – and decrease the stress hormone cortisol. It can also lower your blood pressure, so it's time to relax at the end of the day with a comedy DVD or go and see your favourite comedian.

27. How to motivate your colleagues

You are stressed because you find it difficult, if not impossible, to motivate your colleagues (who may be reporting to you). Their performance has fallen short of what's required. What can you do to increase their motivation and reduce your stress? You need to remember you cannot motivate your colleagues – they need to motivate themselves.

Nevertheless, you have to find out what your colleagues want from their work – the motivators. If they have these, hopefully their motivation will increase; if they do not, their motivation will decrease or, if you're lucky, remain static. How can you find out what employees want from work? One way is to ask them to complete a questionnaire.

In 1946 the Labor Relations Institute of New York (now known as the Office of Labor Relations) asked employees and their managers what these factors were. The top ten items most desired by employees, according to managers, were:

1. Good wages

2. Job security

3. Promotion/growth opportunities

4. Good working conditions

5. Interesting work

6. Personal loyalty to workers

7. Tactful discipline

8. Full appreciation for work done

9. Sympathetic help with personal problems

10. Feeling 'in' on things

Is this roughly what you believe? What you believe will determine how you behave towards your colleagues. Do you think if you give workers pay rise this would improve their motivation? It won't. Counter to what managers perceived, this is what employees actually said about what was important to them:

1. Full appreciation for work done

2. Feeling 'in' on things

3. Sympathetic help with personal problems

4. Job security

5. Good wages

6. Interesting work

7. Promotion/growth opportunities

8. Personal loyalty to workers

9. Good working conditions

10. Tactful discipline

This list is quite different from what the managers thought. 'Good wages' comes well down the list. Employees say primarily they want to be appreciated for the work they do. You might think things have changed since 1946, but these lists have been replicated in recent times over the years, with consistently similar results. The 1946 study is still taught to managers and those in charge of others.

Maybe you can't give your co-workers items that will motivate them, but at least you can try to remove those things that demotivate them. What are the demotivators? Nine of them are as follows:

1. Micromanagement of their work – most employees want to work independently

2. Uncertainty of what they are trying to achieve

3. Lack of recognition for a job well done

4. Being given too much work to do

5. Receiving a salary below the equivalent employees are earning elsewhere

6. Lack of flexible working; a flexible approach to the working week is desirable

7. A poor organisational culture

8. Difficulty in maintaining a work–home balance

9. No opportunities to learn and develop themselves

Using the information above you can try to improve the motivation of your colleagues by removing the demotivators. If you personally cannot wield this sort of influence you will need to speak to your boss to suggest the above areas that need consideration.

Chapter 6

The Climate and Culture of your Organisation

28. What to do if the structure of your organisation is causing you stress

Discussing organisation design, *The Wall Street Journal* of 26 October 2009 reported the following:

We've all been there. You want to get something done at work that seems so simple. And yet it ends up being so ... hard. Too many layers, too many rules, too many cooks, too many everything. What's even more frustrating is that those at the top often aren't even aware of the frustrations. After all, they don't have to deal with them. In fact, they often put those complexities there in the first place. So they remain blissfully ignorant of the problems they've created. Until, that is, it's too late. Until the [organisation] is toppling under the weight of its own inefficiencies.

Do you ever get stressed because this happens to you in your organisation? Your ideas have to be approved by your boss, who has to get the approval of their boss, who has to get the approval of a committee, and so on! So you stop coming up with ideas. It may be that the design of the organisation is causing you problems and therefore stress.

Organisation design can be thought of as the formal structure of an organisation. To find out about your company's organisational design, look at the organisational chart. The organisation should be structured in such a way that it provides excellent customer service, increased profitability, has minimal operating costs, operates at maximum efficiency with minimum cycle time, and has committed and engaged employees. When you examine your organisation's design do these points apply?

How do you know if organisational design is causing problems at work?

A poor organisational design, apart from causing you stress, can result in numerous problems including:

 Delays in decision-making – it takes ages to get something done, if it's done at all.

 A lack of trust between workers and management.

 Poor or little focus on the customer.

A mentality that produces 'silos' and 'turf wars'. A silo mentality occurs when several departments or groups do not want to share information or knowledge with others in the same company. A silo mentality reduces efficiency and can be a contributing factor to a failing corporate culture. A turf war occurs when people say 'it's the marketing department's work' or 'my department should get the resources, not yours'.

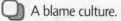 The 'it's not my job' syndrome.

A blame culture.

What can you about it?

Tell your boss about the benefits of good organisational design. It's best to mention this casually or in passing. You could say that good organisational design improves communications, productivity and innovation – an organisation where people can work effectively. On the other hand, although a company has great employees and leaders, a poor organisational design can mean it does not perform well.

If the current organisational design is causing you too many problems and you can't get it changed, you may have to deal with the status quo. For instance, if your organisation is multi-layered and decisions are hard to come by, and you can see no way you can personally improve the decision-making process, you need to find personal strategies for coping. These personal strategies are mentioned throughout this book, but here are a few that you might use: develop a network of people, learn new skills that will help you if you want to leave your present job, be optimistic about life, do exercise and make sure you have interests outside work.

29. How to increase your commitment to the organisation

How strong is your commitment to the organisation you work for? Do you accept the organisation's goals and values? Are you willing to expend a lot of effort for the organisation? Do you want to stay in your current job? These are some of the factors that will help determine if you are committed to the organisation. If you're committed and you have adequate job experience, it has been shown that you will perform better and make any stress that you may have work for you. The reverse occurs if you have a lower level of commitment and weaker job experience, and your stress can make your performance poorer.

Maybe you're a school teacher; your commitment (and intention of leaving) depends on your belief that you are competent, the amount of stress that the job gives you and the environment in which you have to work. This may be true of other jobs as well (it's also been found in blue-collar roles). One study found that if you suffer from stress you feel less emotionally committed to the organisation and if you have yet more stress to deal with, your sense of belonging is reduced (although you might still stay in the job). Stress, in other words, affects your commitment to the organisation you work for.

To find out if you are committed to your organisation, take this test, scoring each as follows.

7 = it's definitely true of me

6 = it's generally true of me

5 = it's often true of me

4 = it's sometimes true and sometimes it's not true of me

3 = it's often untrue of me

2 = it's generally untrue of me

1 = it's definitely true of me

1. I am willing to work harder when required.

2. I would leave the organisation if a similar job came up elsewhere*.

3. I have very little loyalty to the organisation*.

4. I would take almost any job so that I might stay in the organisation.

5. My values and the organisation's values are pretty much the same.

6. I am very proud to tell people I work for this organisation.

7. I am glad I work here, because I could have gone elsewhere.

For the two items marked with a * deduct your score from 8 to get a new score. Add up your final scores. If you scored 35 to 49, you are committed to the organisation – the higher the score the more committed you are. If you scored 7 to 21 you are not committed to the organisation – the lower the score the less committed you are.

How does it happen?

 The organisation has changed for the worse since you joined.

 You feel as if you are working in the wrong kind of organisation.

 For many reasons, you have lost any loyalty to the organisation.

 The organisation has let you down badly.

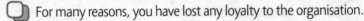 Your organisation has been taken over by another company with a different culture.

How do you know if your commitment to the organisation is causing you stress?

 The organisation doesn't value you or your work.

 You are in permanent state of stress at work, which is caused by the organisation.

What can you do about it?

 Support the organisation's mission and ideals – look at mission statements, annual reports, etc., to help you fully understand what these are. Once you have understood the organisation's values you need to reflect on your own values. If there is little to no overlap you need to consider if you are working for the right organisation – because it is unlikely you will ever feel you fit in and this will cause you further stress.

Embrace change. If you can see there is some synergy between your values and those of the organisation, but there are areas of divergence, you can look at any areas you can work on to change.

Show you hold the values of the department. You can do this by exhibiting a strong work ethic – that you are dependable and responsible, honest, adaptable and trustworthy, and that you are loyal to the department and organisation. These are what employers look for in their employees and they will help you to progress in the organisation.

Support the decisions made by your organisation and speak positively about it outside of the work. Do not be surprised that what you say about the organisation gets back to your boss and managers, and if it's negative it may be held against you. So be careful about what you say.

30. How to change the organisational culture

Is the organisation in which you work supportive and open? This is a major aspect of the organisational culture. Organisational culture is like the 'personality' of an organisation. It affects the way we think, the way we speak to others in the organisation, what we tell others about the organisation and our attitude towards it, the atmosphere found there and so on. It's the way employees usually behave at work. Organisational culture determines how buildings are used, the furniture in them, the clothes employees wear, the symbols found in the organisation, etc. Organisational culture is determined by the people at the top and by the employees.

It has been said that the culture of an organisation is the single most important factor accounting for success or failure. Organisational culture, when it's healthy, produces good performance from employees and keeps stress levels lower. When organisational culture is bad, employees get frustrated and stressed. Which kind of organisational culture do you work in?

The existence of competition in an organisation, due to, for instance, downsizing and budget cuts, develops stress in the form of job insecurity, work overload, difficulties in obtaining promotion, competition within and between groups, and an under-utilisation of staff skills.

Here are some of the items you might consider in order to determine if the organisation's culture is causing you stress:

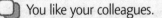 Staff are treated fairly depending on their performance.

Staff are treated with no favouritism.

You can disagree with your manager and it is not held against you.

 Absenteeism is not a problem.

People here are well qualified to do the work.

 You like your colleagues.

Managers try to achieve their objectives.

 Meetings are open and everyone is encouraged to contribute.

Those chosen to work in the organisation have good qualifications.

You enjoy the company of your colleagues.

Your managers show the drive to achieve.

How does it happen?

Your organisation is taken over by or merged with another whose culture is quite different.

The owners or bosses of the organisation set the (negative) culture.

The (new) technology your organisation uses changes the organisational culture.

How do you know if the organisational culture is affecting you?

You disagree with certain aspects of the organisational culture.

You are frustrated by poor communication in the organisation.

The leader of your department or organisation has a neurotic style and this is affecting you. Dr Kurt Motamedi, professor of strategy and leadership at Pepperdine University in the USA, believes that the neurotic management styles of key managers dominate the organisation's culture and norms. Employees are berated, dismissed or left to their own devices without direction. When people find themselves in a neurotic culture, feelings of insecurity become pervasive and employees feel emotionally abused and abandoned.

 Your organisation has a poor reputation and it is difficult to recruit suitable candidates.

Your organisation (and you, perhaps) is affected by absenteeism, stress and disability.

Bullying and harassment are tolerated within the organisation.

What can you do about it?

If your organisation is taken over by or merged with another whose culture is quite different, ask your boss if you can:

Have a meeting to discuss any differences between your organisation and the new order. If not, this can be done via newsletter or anything that will inform employees about what is going on.

Decide if you will compromise or accept the current organisational culture. For this, you have to understand the culture of the organisation. In order to find out about the culture of an organisation you should walk around your department and look at how the space is divided, if there are any common areas, who gets the best offices, what's on the walls, etc. If you can, you could talk to staff and ask them what it's like working there; enquire about the information and feedback they get from their bosses; and how the organisation deals with new staff (what training they get, whether they are introduced to colleagues, and so on). The organisation should provide training, especially for new staff, about the culture of the organisation.

If you talk to like-minded colleagues you can set up a subculture in your department. A subculture is a set of values shared by a minority, usually a small minority, of an organisation's members. These often occur in departments where members have had to face distinctive problems and have a wealth of shared experiences. Of course, you have to be certain that your subculture is acceptable to the organisation as a whole.

31. Office politics and how to cope with it

Office politics is quite normal – it is basic human nature operating in the workplace. If you're working with other people, as you're likely to, then you will encounter office politics. It comes from competition among employees for things such as money and promotions. It also is based upon the personalities of some people.

Office politics is more than just disliking some people at work. It refers to the use and acquisition of power outside of the employee's job requirements. The outcomes the employee is pursuing by the use of office politics, or the means by which the outcomes are sought, or both, would not be approved by the organisation. Office politics can cause stress for colleagues and can result in conflict within the organisation. A recent survey of almost 500 managers found that conflict in the workplace had increased, and 44 per cent of them believed office politics was the main cause of this increase.

Maybe you are stressed because a colleague is using office politics to advance themselves; looking at dealers in the London money market, it was found that more than 45 per cent felt coping with office politics was a stressful work-related item. Many managers who play at office politics cause their staff stress. It has been said that office politics determines promotions, transfers, supplies, equipment, who is in charge of what and how managers liaise with each other. One psychologist said if you have more than one employee, you've got office politics – it will determine who gets a pay increase or a better job. Another management researcher noted that if you try to ignore office politics, then you're a fool. The research further highlighted that underperforming organisations are more likely to experience an increase in political behaviour as well as viewing such behaviour as a source of conflict.

How does it happen?

 You have to work with someone who knows how office politics operates.

 You don't think you can maintain your credibility and beliefs if you indulge in office politics.

What can you do about it?

If you're an employee, use techniques that will help you when in competition with colleagues:

 Build an image of success by being associated with successful projects and individuals. Emphasise successes and don't mention your failures.

 Create obligations in others. Do favours for those who might help you in future by returning your favour.

Establish relationships with powerful people. Find a mentor who is important and influential in the organisation.

Always give excellent performance. Go beyond the job you have, volunteer for demanding and unpopular projects.

Talk positively about the organisation and department you work for.

Endeavour to be known as knowledgeable and keep an ear out for information that might be useful for your role.

Develop a network of relationships throughout the organisation. You can use modern technology to build up a network of people that can help you at work (and maybe when you want to get a new job).

Manage your boss. Understand their aims, goals, strengths, weaknesses, blind spots, pressures and preferred work style. Keep your boss informed and be careful with their (limited) time; give them help and support.

Remember the expression 'keep your friends close and your enemies closer'? This is very relevant to office politics. To those you regard as your 'enemies' you should always be pleasant, but be careful what you say to them. Find out what motivates them and from this you can learn how to avoid their unfriendly muckraking.

If you're an employer or manager:

 Team building is a good way to prevent the negative effects of office politics. People have to work together in order to successfully complete a project.

Whatever your position in the organisation:

 Don't gossip or spread rumours, don't get involved with others' arguments, don't complain and maintain your integrity at all times.

Sometimes you will have to protect yourself from others. You might select one or more of the following defensive but negative behaviours (which you might later come to regret because you are associated with them):

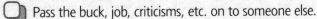 Pass the buck, job, criticisms, etc. on to someone else.

 Plead ignorance or lack of skills.

 Support an action in public (and do as little as possible in private).

 Appear to be so busy that you cannot support your colleague.

These are unprofessional and may not enhance your integrity.

32. How to deal with favouritism in the workplace

It won't be a surprise to you. Nepotism, cronyism and favouritism occur in many organisations, and are used to give preferential treatment to relatives and friends in employment. One study showed that nepotism, cronyism and favouritism created job stress within the workplace, and nepotism was found to be the biggest factor in creating job stress.

Favouritism happens when the manager, boss or leader displays preferential treatment towards those workers with whom they are connected in some way. This negatively affects other employees and possibly the overall performance of the organisation. It can be completely demotivating to staff. Favouritism in the workplace means that someone – or a group – is treated better than others and the reason is not necessarily related to superior work performance. The person who is favoured might be promoted faster than others, get more for doing the same job, be granted more freedom than others, etc.

As the result of favouritism, your boss might:

 Spend more time with the chosen employee.

 Confide in the favourite employee.

 Discuss confidential issues with the employee.

 Overlook any of the employee's mistakes.

 Listen to and follow the employee's advice.

One study in the USA found that nearly 40 per cent of employees felt there was favouritism within their department.

What can you do about it?

For employees:

Talk to the human resources department in your organisation or to a manager you can trust. Make it clear what you are worried about, and give them any relevant information about the occurrences of favouritism. Ask human resources or the manager what you should do while your claim is being checked. At the same time, ensure you are performing to the best of your ability so the favouritism you claim is not mistaken for the other colleague simply performing better than you.

For employers, to ensure there is no favouritism in the organisation:

○ Inspect your organisation's methods of selection and promotion.

○ Have mentors for minority staff.

○ Ensure that any advancement and perks are based on performance.

○ Do not support husbands and wives, etc., working in the same department or even in the same organisation.

Don't get caught up

Don't get caught up in forming a grudge against your colleagues. The 'favourite' may be unaware of preferential treatment; reserve your judgement and energy for the company's investigation into your claim.

33. How to make sure there is no discrimination in your workplace

Do you feel you have been discriminated against at work because you're a member of a minority group? Does it cause you stress every day you go to work? Everyday discrimination is defined as the subtle acts that are experienced by members of a group (racial, religious, national) on a daily basis. Does this fit in with how you feel?

Discrimination can cause stress. In the UK it has been shown that black African-Caribbean respondents reported higher work stress than either Bangladeshi or white respondents, and that racial discrimination among black African-Caribbean female respondents resulted in greater perceived work stress and higher levels of psychological distress.

The UK government has said 'it's unlawful for an employer to discriminate against you because of your race. You are protected against racial discrimination at all stages of employment' and 'the Equality Act 2010 makes it unlawful for an employer to discriminate against you because of race. Race includes colour, nationality, and ethnic or national origins. Under the Act, it doesn't matter if the discrimination is on purpose or not. What counts is whether (as a result of an employer's actions) you are treated less favourably than someone else because of race. The Equality Act 2010 protects all racial groups, regardless of their race, colour, nationality, or national or ethnic origins. The laws against racial discrimination at work cover every part of employment. This includes recruitment, terms and conditions, pay and benefits, status, training, promotion and transfer opportunities, right through to redundancy and dismissal'.

You can't be discriminated against because of your:

 Gender

 Marriage or civil partnership

 Gender reassignment

 Pregnancy and maternity leave

 Sexual orientation

 Disability

 Race

 Colour

 Ethnic background

 Nationality

Religion or belief

Age

That's the UK law.

You might be suffering from one or more of the four major types of racial discrimination – direct discrimination (where, for example, race is an effective cause for less favourable treatment); indirect discrimination (rules or policies are imposed on everyone but which particularly disadvantage members of a particular group if that cannot be justified); harassment (participating in, allowing or encouraging unwanted behaviour that offends someone or creates a hostile atmosphere, for instance, making racist jokes at work); or victimisation (treating someone badly because they have complained or supported someone bringing a complaint about discrimination).

What you can do if you suspect you've been discriminated against

The UK government suggests that if it's another employee who is the source of the problem you should talk to your immediate boss and explain your concerns. If it's your boss who is discriminating against you, you should talk to their boss or to the company's human resources department. If your employer won't help, then you may need to make a complaint using your employer's grievance procedure.

Don't forget your trade union official may be able to help you, and make sure you know the current law concerning racial discrimination before you make a complaint.

Maybe you feel you have been subject to sexual discrimination. You believe you are doing the same work as a colleague and getting paid less, or are being discriminated against in some other way because of your sex. The UK government is quite clear about this:

Under the Equality Act 2010 it's unlawful for an employer to discriminate against you because of your sex. Sex discrimination law covers almost all workers (men and women) and all types of organisations in the UK. It covers recruitment, employment terms and conditions, pay and benefits, training, promotion and transfer opportunities, redundancy and dismissal. If you believe that you are being paid less than a colleague who's doing the same job, then you can refer to the rules about equal terms and equal pay. Where men and women, working for the same employer, are doing one of the following they are entitled to the same terms in their employment contract: the same or similar work, work rated as equivalent in a job evaluation study by the employer, and work of equal value.

What you can do if you think you are being discriminated against because of your sex

You can talk or write to your employer, and if they won't help you may be able to take your case to an employment tribunal. You can also contact ACAS (the Advisory, Conciliation & Arbitration Service) and your trade union. Again, make sure you know the current law about sexual discrimination.

There are other forms of discrimination in the workplace, and they may be subject to different laws: age discrimination, disability discrimination, and religious or belief discrimination. Whatever the discrimination, they can all cause you stress.

34. How to deal with violence at work

Don't be surprised if you have witnessed or experienced violence at work. A recent report showed that across the EU an average of 5 per cent of employees reported being the subject of physical violence –

from a colleague. The figure was even worse in the UK, at around 9 per cent. Both being a victim of physical assault and simply seeing violence at work can result in trauma. The fear of workplace violence can result in anxiety and a desire to leave the organisation.

If you're a taxi driver, you know all about violence at work. The murder rate associated with occupations in the USA, measured per 100,000 workers, is the highest for taxi drivers – who are four times more likely to be murdered at work than police officers or other law enforcement workers. In the West Midlands in the UK, recorded crime statistics in 2010 showed a fivefold increase of violent attacks on taxi drivers since 2000, and that feedback from taxi driver and operator associations shows the West Midlands figures are far from being an isolated trend.

Hopefully you're not a taxi driver but you may have witnessed or experienced violence at your place of work. It seems those jobs that are subject to violence have certain features in common: employees encounter members of the public, they handle cash, staff work alone or in small numbers, employees work early in the morning or late at night, and the premises they work in are relatively unsecured and tend to be located in depressed areas. The major factors that can result in violence in the workplace are as dealing with the public, denying someone a service, making decisions that affect other people, having to supervise and discipline others, working in a job that involves the security of premises, having to work with valuable items, working at night or at weekends, working alone, doing a job that involves alcohol, being a care worker and going into other people's homes. So if you are working in a job that contains more of these factors you have a greater chance of encountering violence at work. For instance, as well as taxi drivers, it has been suggested that psychiatric nurses encounter more workplace violence than other nurses. Psychiatric nurses work in a job that attracts many of these factors and this also applies to 'ordinary' nurses.

What you can do about eliminating the prospect of violence at work

For employers, the possibility of violence at work can be reduced by:

Using stress reduction programmes, as stress is regarded as a major source of violent behaviour. Stress reduction programmes – or stress management programmes – are often offered by an organisation's human resources department. These generally consist of indicating what the major sources of stress at work are, how to recognise stress in yourself and others, and how to increase your resilience to stress. The main aim of these courses is to examine the effects of stress and to encourage the individual to develop a personal stress-control plan. If you want more information on stress reduction or stress management programmes there are numerous references online, or you can contact a local EAP or stress management consultancy.

Improving employment screening – using psychometric tests and background checks to determine who might be prone to violence.

Ensuring that the organisation's non-harassment policies are implemented.

Making use of EAPs.

Educating employees about the causes of workplace violence.

For employees, violence at work can cause pain, suffering and even disability or death. Physical attacks are obviously dangerous, but serious or persistent verbal abuse or threats can also damage employees' health through anxiety or stress. What can you do if you witness or are the victim of violence at work?

◯ Report it to the human resources department.

◯ If you don't have a human resources department or equivalent then report it immediately to your supervisor or a higher authority.

◯ If it is your supervisor, boss or owner who is the cause of the violence, and you don't have a human resources department, then you should take legal action.

◯ In all these cases, ensure that appropriate action is taken.

If violence at work does occur then the victim or witness may suffer from post-traumatic stress disorder (PTSD). Post-traumatic stress disorder is a psychiatric disorder that can occur following the experience or witnessing of life-threatening events, such as military combat, natural disasters, terrorist incidents, serious accidents or violent personal assaults. The symptoms of PTSD can include reliving the experience through nightmares and flashbacks, difficulty sleeping, and feeling detached or estranged, and these symptoms can be severe enough and last long enough to significantly impair the individual's daily life.

How can PTSD be treated? Treatment for PTSD comes in a variety of forms of psychotherapy and drug therapy. There is no definitive treatment, and no cure, but some treatments appear to be quite promising, especially cognitive behavioural therapy, group therapy and exposure therapy, in which the patient repeatedly relives the frightening experience under controlled conditions to help them work through the trauma. Anyone who suspects they are suffering from PTSD should consult a medical professional.

35. How to cope with political correctness in the workplace

Are you unsure about political correctness? Do you worry you might say the wrong thing to a colleague? Are you afraid to criticise one of your employees because you're afraid you'll be accused of discrimination? Do you fear offending someone and losing your job, or getting yourself or your employer sued?

Well, one of the authors of this book understands exactly what you are going through. Some time ago he had to examine a dissertation written by a student at a different university. It was a poor piece of work that he was asked to review, and the author of the dissertation was given some advice on its failings and how they should be corrected so that a resubmission would obtain a pass mark. On receiving the poor score, the student threatened to take the examiner to a tribunal and to sue his university. The basis of the student's case was that the examiner was biased against the student because he was from a minority ethnic group. The examiner was completely oblivious to the origins of the student. The case was quietly dropped, and the student resubmitted the dissertation and was awarded a pass. For a short period of time, the examiner was very concerned about the potential of the case.

What is meant by political correctness? Political correctness (PC) describes language, ideas, policies and behaviour that reduce any social and institutional offence in occupational, gender, racial, cultural, sexual orientation, religion, beliefs or ideologies, disability and age-related environments. On the other hand, many people see PC as having the potential to be something more invidious:

 Doing the reverse of what common sense would suggest.

 Inconveniencing the innocent while making life easier for the wrongdoer.

 Not telling the truth in case it offends.

 Changing your language where you perceive it may offend.

 Doing exactly the opposite of what you preach.

 What you do has the effect of making the problem you were trying to cure far worse.

 Doing ridiculous things just for a political reason.

Favouring a minority just for a political reason.

You'll have to judge for yourself which version of PC is acceptable to you.

How to be politically correct

The main thing you have to do is to learn about other people and cultures. If you do that you can then:

Be careful how you use humour. You might think you're being funny but you might be offending other people.

Get rid of your assumptions of other people. Think about why you have (usually negative) views about the people in a particular group. Once you have done that you can remove these hurtful ideas.

Make friends with people from different cultures. You'll be amazed how much you have in common, especially when it comes to the organisation you both work in.

Mind your language. Different cultures have different ways of talking to each other, which you might not be familiar with. They may also differ in how they employ body language, non-verbal cues, communication style, etc.

You might also want to attend a course run by your organisation, or an external agency, which will help you to be aware of other groups and how you can improve your relationships with them.

36. How you can get the organisation to be more committed to you

Do you have the feeling that the organisation you work for is not on your side and does not support you? Meanwhile, you give your best and are committed to the organisation. If so, it's not surprising that you get stressed. If you believe you don't get the support from the organisation that you need, this can cause you to have lots of psychological problems and your performance may drop off. You may also think of leaving the company. Numerous investigations have shown that employees believe their organisation has a general positive or negative orientation towards them. This orientation is both to their contributions and their welfare.

Complete this short questionnaire (developed by the University of Delaware) to determine if you think your organisation is committed to you. Listed below are some statements that represent possible opinions you may have about working in your organisation. Indicate the degree of your agreement or disagreement with each statement by giving each a score as follows:

1 = Strongly disagree

2 = Moderately disagree

3 = Slightly disagree

4 = Neither agree nor disagree

5 = Slightly agree

6 = Moderately agree

7 = Strongly agree

1. The organisation values my contribution to its well-being.

2. The organisation fails to appreciate any extra effort from me (R).

3. The organisation would ignore any complaint from me (R).

4. The organisation really cares about my well-being.

5. Even if I did the best job possible, the organisation would fail to notice (R).

6. The organisation cares about my general satisfaction at work.

7. The organisation shows very little concern for me (R).

8. The organisation takes pride in my accomplishments at work.

Those statements marked (R) are reverse-scored. This means you subtract your original score from 8. Now add all your scores.

If you scored between 8 and 16, you feel you are not receiving the support and commitment you require from the organisation.

If you scored 17–40, you are getting some support and commitment from the organisation.

If you scored 41–56, you feel you are receiving the support and commitment you require from the organisation.

If you believe you are not getting the commitment you need, the above statements will help to show where the problems lie. You can then ask your boss to remedy the failings. For instance, if you scored very low (after you have reverse-scored your original score) on statement 3, you can find out what happens to your complaints, who is not replying to you and why. You can then attempt to have the system for handling complaints changed.

What can you do about it?

If you want to increase your organisation's commitment to you, you need to appreciate the qualities the organisation looks for in its employees. These include punctuality, honesty, an ability to handle pressure, dependability, efficiency and creativity, as well as doing a good job. You should ensure that you meet all of these requirements.

Chapter 7

Work–Life Balance

37. Use flexible working to improve your work–life balance

There is little doubt that flexible working can increase productivity and improve work–life balance, as well as reduce the stress levels of employees. It's said that flexible working is good for businesses, families, older workers, carers and a growing population who want a better balance between home and work life. The National Institute for Health & Clinical Excellence (NICE) in the UK has reported that, in order to improve the psychological health of employees, organisations should introduce flexible working conditions where it is reasonably practical. This could be part-time, home-based, flexitime or job sharing, and these are likely to improve employees' perceptions of control, as well as promote engagement and job satisfaction. Requests for flexible working should be considered consistently and fairly by the organisation.

Flexible working can also include other forms of alternative work arrangements, such as leave of absence, telecommuting, compressed working hours, staggered working hours, shift working, self-scheduling, time off in lieu, term-time working, annual hours, etc. About half of large businesses encourage flexible and remote working and around 43 per cent of UK organisations identify higher productivity as the key benefit of flexible working.

The UK government states that anyone can ask their employer for flexible work arrangements, and the law provides some employees with the statutory right to request a flexible working pattern. Though there are requirements for the employee to meet, you have the statutory right if you have or expect to have parental responsibility of a child aged under 17; have or expect to have parental responsibility of a disabled child under 18 who receives disability living allowance (DLA); are the parent/guardian/special guardian/foster parent/ private foster carer or are the holder of a residence order; or the spouse, partner or civil partner of one of these and are applying to care for the child; or if you are a carer who cares, or expects to be caring, for an adult who is a spouse, partner, civil partner or relative, or who, although not related to you, lives at the same address as you. To read a summary of the legal aspects of flexible working practices, and the employer's obligations, look at www.gov.uk/flexible-working.

Under the law, you have the right to ask for flexible working – not the right to have it. Employers can reasonably decline your application where there is a legitimate business reason.

Remember that there are disadvantages to flexible working. You might not feel part of a team if you're not in the office every day, you could miss out on establishing friendships with your work colleagues because you won't see them as much as you might, you may miss out on promotions and if you're working from home you might be tempted not to stop! The price of flexible working is that you tend to do more work than you are paid for.

How does it happen?

 Employees argue successfully that they should have flexitime.

 Management accepts that flexible working will be beneficial to the organisation and to the staff.

 The trade union(s) involved request flexible working for staff.

 Similar organisations offer flexible working and this affects staff recruitment.

 The organisation wants to attract employees, such as mothers with young children, who require flexible working.

 Older staff, who are ready to wind down their career, do not want to completely retire.

How do you know when you need flexible working?

 You are part of a dual-career family and relations with your partner or family are fraught.

 Technology allows you to work anywhere, at any time, etc., and this looks attractive.

 Changes in your personal life mean it would be helpful if the organisation offered flexible working.

 You want to balance work–home life.

○ You want to improve your quality of life, reduce stress and increase your job satisfaction.

○ The organisation wants to keep staff, increase productivity, decrease absence, support diversity, etc.

What can you do about it?

○ Speak to your manager. You'll have to put together a reasonable business case to backup your request. For instance, you'll need to look at what work needs to be done, how it could be transferred, if the organisation would need more staff to cover your flexible working, etc.

○ Approach your trade union for support.

○ Check your legal rights before you ask your organisation for flexible working.

Not all jobs lend themselves to flexible working and providing suitable technology can be expensive for the employer. You may feel socially isolated and your boss may find it difficult to communicate with you. Your career development and training may suffer, health and safety issues, and the recording of the number of hours you have worked may also be problematic. If you really want flexible working you should consider a career in retailing, working at home, self-employment, etc.

38. How to cope with travelling to and from work

Travel has always been stressful, but in recent years there has been an increase in airport security, there is more traffic on the road and the trains are fuller than ever – sometimes you can't even get a seat. It has been found that nearly one in three UK drivers experiences stress. A World Bank study reported that insurance claims for health problems tend to increase among employees who travel often and employees who travel overseas are twice as likely to file health claims for psychological problems (male travellers are 80 per cent and female travelling executives are 18 per cent more likely to file such claims). Perhaps you have to travel as part of your job, either locally, countrywide or internationally – and it may be making you ill.

Unfortunately, with travel, things can slip out of our control. You know what it's like to come to a standstill because a set of traffic lights has broken down, or you might be held up at the airport if your plane has been delayed. A simple car journey can be blighted by roadworks. Research has shown that driving a car is significantly more stressful than travelling by bus – results indicated that stress was, on average, 33 per cent lower when travelling by bus. Another survey of motorists found that 25 per cent admitted they got easily bored while driving and 22 per cent of drivers regularly went into 'autopilot'. Men have been found to suffer a significant and unhealthy increase in psychological stress when driving in traffic when compared with women. It was found that women suffered an 8.7 per cent increase in stress from driving in traffic, while men suffered an increase of 60 per cent. The same research showed that drivers may suffer from physical symptoms such as dizziness, breathlessness, muscular aches and chest pains, while their behavioural symptoms include agitation and erratic driving.

Women travellers suffer from particular stresses. If you are travelling to certain countries with a different culture from that you are used to, you need to be aware of possible sexual harassment. Thieves often see women as easy targets, so don't wear expensive jewellery, carry a torch, and avoid dark streets. In some cultures women drivers, and women travelling alone, are unusual.

How does it happen?

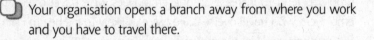 Your organisation opens a branch away from where you work and you have to travel there.

Ⓓ You have to travel by road, etc., to get to work.

Ⓓ You are promoted and this requires you to undertake travelling.

Ⓓ Your job entails travelling to visit clients.

How do you know if travelling for work is causing you stress?

Ⓓ You become more nervous than usual when you're driving, and you do not look forward to travelling by bus, car, aeroplane or train.

Ⓓ You are tired when you arrive at your destination and you have little or no time to recover because there is a meeting you must attend.

Ⓓ Your home and social life are suffering because travelling takes up all your spare time.

You are accident-prone when you're travelling by car. Some people are simply involved in accidents even when they're driving safely and are following the rules.

What can you do about it?

If you have a long or complicated journey, planning ahead will help relieve stress. The more organised you can be the less stress you will encounter. If you are travelling by aeroplane, you can:

 Arrange your travel to and from the airport in advance.

 Arrive at the airport in plenty of time.

 Check in online.

Remember to leave enough time to go through security.

Purchase any articles you want before you get on the plane.

Do recommended exercises at your seat or walk around.

If you are driving, you can:

 Drive smoothly – avoid sharp acceleration and braking.

 Keep the engine in good technical condition.

Keep the car tyres inflated to the recommended pressures.

Use the car's air conditioning wisely. If it's warm and humid outside and you have been chilled by the air conditioning you'll get a shock when you get out of the car.

 Take regular breaks.

However you're travelling:

 Stay hydrated by drinking lots of water.

Ask yourself if your work could be carried out remotely, either from home or the office, and avoid you having to travel. A remote worker who spends two days a week at home has been found to save eight hours on travel.

Arrange accommodation well in advance.

Write a travel agenda.

Add some contingency time to your estimated travelling time.

39. How to keep your work and personal life separate

Do you feel that your work is interfering with your home and social life? Do you find your life outside the organisation is affecting your work? Or both? Do you think that because of work you cannot lead a fulfilling life? Whereas in the 1970s you might have been working a 40-hour (or fewer) week, now you may have to work at home, on your computer. Some jobs require your attention round the clock, for instance, lawyers, bankers, academics, some public servants. For many employees there is no escape from work. Maybe you are on call 24 hours a day – technology allows you to work from almost anywhere in the world and your organisation may require you to work from anywhere. Many employees are part of a dual-career couple, where both partners are working.

Some research has shown that workers are more concerned with their work–life balance than their job security. To help this concern, many organisations have introduced creches, flexitime, remote working, and part-time work. Many younger employees say choosing a job is dependent on the organisation's family-friendly attitude.

Conflict between work and family/social life is bad for the well-being of the individual. If this conflict occurs it has been recorded that the affected employees have lower job satisfaction, high emotional exhaustion and want to leave the organisation. It has also been suggested that such employees are 30 times more likely to suffer a mental health problem such as depression or anxiety, and work-home conflict can result in worsening relationships between partners.

It has been found that part-time workers are less stressed than those who work from home. However, if you work at home you tend to work for more hours than you are paid for. You also find yourself answering the door and your phone, picking up emails, reading your post, making a coffee, etc. So don't always think working at home will be the answer!

Does your organisation have a family-friendly policy?

Try this questionnaire. For each statement score your answer using the following scale:

5 = Very much so

4 = Most of the time

3 = Neutral

2 = Not most of the time

1 = No, never

1. I have flexible starting times.

2. When there is a family crisis I can get time off.

3. I can have time off in the school holidays.

4. I have flexible finishing times.

5. My performance is the main factor to my boss, not my 'face time'.

6. My organisation lets me do my work at home.

7. My boss is sympathetic to my family needs.

If your total score is between 7 and 14 your organisation is not very 'family friendly'.

If your total score is between 28 and 35 your organisation appears to be 'family friendly'.

How does it happen?

Your organisation has reduced its staff numbers.

Your organisation is not adhering to the law regarding employees' rights.

 There has been a major change in your life outside work.

 You have been promoted or transferred at work.

How do you know if work is affecting your family/social life?

 Your performance at work has deteriorated.

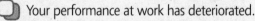 There is less time to communicate with your partner/family.

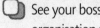 You communicate negatively with people at work.

 Your social life has deteriorated.

What can you do about it?

 See your boss and tell them about the advantages of having an organisation that offers family-friendly policies, such as:

 Nursery places at work

Childcare vouchers

Flexible working hours

Opportunity to work remotely

If you can't or don't want to change your job, you may need to consider that for the greater good of your heath and relationship with your family or partner something will have to give. You might have to reduce your salary by taking on part-time work or a lower-paying job that offers you what you need. You need to make sure time is made for relaxation outside of work and make a concerted effort to allot a special day at the weekend that is sacrosanct for family time.

Unplug

Avoid taking your work home with you. Disable email alerts on your phone or tablet, or, if it is company-issued, switch it off altogether. Avoid checking your emails on your home devices as well. If you must take work home with you, schedule it into your evening and don't allow it to overrun into family time.

Chapter 8

Personal strategies

In this chapter we offer some methods that can help you reduce your stress. Work is stressful – it's that simple. If you want to stay healthy and enjoy a more stress-free life, you should eat healthily. Certain foods can help reduce blood pressure and cholesterol, and there are also foods that are recommended to reduce stress levels. This is not a book about food, but many nutritionists believe the Mediterranean diet can help reduce your stress. This diet concentrates on plant foods and healthy fats such as omega-3 found in fish. The Mediterranean diet emphasises fruit, vegetables, beans, nuts, seeds and wholegrains.

You can refer to www.shapeonline.com and www.foodnetwork.com, as well as reading US magazine *Better Homes & Gardens* (www.bhg.com) – they all give you healthy recipes.

There are certain foods you should avoid if you want to reduce your stress levels. Caffeine, alcohol, salty foods, hydrogenated fats and glutamates should be avoided in large amounts.

In the remainder of this chapter we suggest some techniques you can use to help manage your stress.

40. Use your breathing to cope with stress

When you're under stress, you tend to breathe through your upper chest and your breaths are short, shallow and rapid.

What you have to do is try and change your upper chest breathing to breathing through your abdomen. Chest breathing is inefficient because most of your blood flow happens in the lower parts of the lungs. However, these parts expand only the minimum when you breathe through your chest. If your breaths are rapid and shallow, and through your upper chest, less oxygen will be transferred to the blood and, consequently, nutrients are not delivered to the tissues as adequately as possible.

If you practise abdomen breathing you will breathe from the abdomen even while you are asleep.

- First of all, sit or stand in a quiet, relaxing place. You'll need about ten minutes by yourself.

- After sitting or standing comfortably, lift up your ribs so that you can make your chest bigger. Breathe through your nose, not your mouth. Put one hand on your chest and put the other on your abdomen. You'll find your abdomen just under your rib cage.

- Take deep, slow, breaths so that they fill your abdomen, not your chest. Count to five as you are breathing in and count to eight as you breathe out.

Breathing through your abdomen affects your autonomic nervous system. This, in turn, results in a range of health benefits. The autonomic nervous system controls all the automatic functions of the body such as digestion, breathing, heart rate, digestion and so on.

41. Control your stress by using biofeedback

Biofeedback is a technique that helps to improve your health by controlling certain bodily processes. These processes occur quite normally and automatically. With biofeedback you can bring certain bodily functions under voluntary control. These include:

 Brainwaves

 Heart rate

 Muscle tension

Stomach acidity

Blood pressure

Skin temperature

These are all affected negatively when you're under stress, so it's worth considering biofeedback as a potential remedy for stress.

If you decide to use biofeedback you may need to consult a qualified practitioner. If you do so, what can you expect? The practitioner may place electrodes on your skin – these won't harm you in any way. The electrodes send data from your body to a monitoring box. There, the data is converted to a variable tone, or a meter, or a computer screen that shows lines moving across a grid, or something similar. The therapist then asks you to carry out mental exercises. After a while you will learn which mental activities will result in the changes you want:

 Brainwaves that you associate with feeling calm.

 Heart rate that is acceptable to you.

 Muscle tension that is normal.

 Stomach acidity that will not result in reflux or the formation of gallstones, etc.

 Blood pressure that is within a safe range.

 Skin temperature that is not increased to a dangerous level.

At the beginning you will use the monitor to see your progress. In the longer term you will be able to control certain bodily functions without the monitor and electrodes. Biofeedback is an effective therapy for many conditions, but it is primarily used to treat high blood pressure, tension headaches, migraines, chronic pain and urinary incontinence – all of which are related to stress and may be caused by the work you are doing.

There are a number of portable devices you can purchase to provide you with the biofeedback you can get from a therapist. Among them are:

 A finger-temperature thermometer. You insert a finger into the equipment and are able to see the effect on you when thinking about a certain topic (your colleagues, boss, the work you have to do, getting to work, etc.).

A heart-rate monitor. You can get feedback on the rate at which your heart is beating by strapping a belt around your chest and a watch-type monitor around your wrist. You can see them being used at your local gym.

The three most common types of biofeedback that your therapist might use are electromyography to measure muscle tension, electroencephalography to measure your brain wave activity, and thermal biofeedback to measure your skin temperature.

Biofeedback is reported as reducing anxiety, controlling both tension and migraine headaches, reducing stress-related hypertension, and modifying type A behaviour (a type A person is ambitious, aggressive, rigidly organised, controlling, highly competitive, status-conscious, arrogant, proactive, obsessed with time management, etc.). It has been demonstrated that biofeedback can help in the treatment of many diseases and painful conditions. It has also been shown that we have more control over so-called involuntary bodily functions than we once thought. But it has also shown that nature limits the extent of such control. Scientists are now trying to determine just how much voluntary control we can exert.

42. Use autogenic training to relax and manage your stress

Autogenic training is a technique you can use to help you relax and manage your stress. You can practise these techniques by yourself and they can be carried out in short bursts of about 15 minutes. You can do them lying down, sitting like a rag doll, or in any relaxing position. In some cases you can do them standing up.

Autogenic training is a method of self-hypnosis (autogenic means self-generation or self-regulation). Autogenic phrases require you to repeat silently one of six phrases. You can use these phrases to help you relax when you feel stressed and you can use them anywhere, anytime. You just say six phrases to yourself. Why not try it. Relax and close your eyes…

First, repeat the following, silently, three times:

 'My right arm is heavy'

 'My left arm is heavy'

 'Both of my arms are heavy'.

You then say these for one leg, then the other leg, then both legs.

Second, repeat the following, silently, three times:

 'My right arm is warm'

 'My left arm is warm'

 'Both of my arms are warm'.

Repeat the above phrases substituting arm for leg, doing the same as you did earlier.

Third, say, silently, 'my heartbeat is regular and calm', five times, slowly.

Fourth, say, silently, 'my breathing is calm and relaxed', five times, slowly.

Fifth, say, silently, 'my solar plexus is warm', five times slowly.

Sixth, say, silently, 'my forehead is cool', five times, slowly.

Repeat the whole sequence of phrases for around 20 minutes.

If you relax your muscles, your mind will automatically follow and you will find yourself in a state of deep relaxation.

You can carry out autogenic training with a qualified teacher and it's best learnt from an experienced clinical psychologist or therapist. You can also buy CDs and DVDs to help you.

After you have mastered self-hypnosis and autogenic training you can start to use other phrases. For instance, to reduce any mental tension you are feeling, you would say: 'I will meet my troubles, calm, collected and cheerful,' and similar phrases. You can also use phrases to deal with any stress you now feel, stress that happened in the past, decisions you have to make, your attempts to reduce smoking, drug and alcohol abuse, slimming, respiration, blushing, etc.

Interestingly, it has been found that one woman who was suffering a migraine attack recovered after her hand temperature rose by 5.5 °C in two minutes, and it has been contended that hand-warming exercises can help cure migraine headaches. If autogenic phrases help you to feel your hands are warmer, they may well get rid of migraine headaches. It has also been reported (of male fire-service employees) that autogenic training improved their heart rate activity and the psychological issues that are affected when they've suffered post-traumatic stress.

43. Talk to yourself (positively) and relieve your stress

Stressors are only negative if you interpret them as threats. Your thinking will affect the way you interpret stressors and the way you think can be negative. In fact, for a lot of people, negative thinking – or negative self-talk – is common. We talk to ourselves (not always out loud) all the time. Examples of negative self-talk are:

- 'I am always given the worst jobs.'

- 'I just cannot convince people of the value of my plans.'

- 'I am no good at making friends at work.'

- 'Workers here are only interested in doing the minimum they can get away with – unlike me.'

- 'I messed up at yesterday's meeting – I am useless.'

- 'I must have everyone's approval that my work is great.'

Now, many of these assertions might be true, but very often you 'see' they are true because you tell yourself they are. It takes time to change the way you think, but it can be done. If, in advance, you can change the way you think, you will be able to manage any stress that comes your way at work. When these negative thoughts occur, ask yourself three questions:

- Is what I am saying to myself true or false?

Am I rushing to judgement?

 What are the outcomes of my self-talk?

Then you can start to give yourself a positive self-talk, using supportive phrases such as:

 'Whatever is happening now will soon pass.'

 'I will not fail.'

 'It is not worth getting upset over this.'

'I will not get angry with this awkward person.'

'I am angry, but I am allowed to be for a short time.'

Once you have learned the technique you can use it to manage your stress – anywhere, as well as at work.

44. How to use progressive relaxation to manage your stress

When you are stressed you often find your muscles become tense and tight. You may be able to reduce your stress by relaxing your muscles; you can do this at work. Recent studies have shown that progressive relaxation can counter the negative effects of stress. Progressive relaxation was used by the US Air Force in World War

Two, to help flight cadets manage their stress, and it is widely used now with positive results.

So how do you do this? It's recommended you find a quiet environment with soft lighting and you'll need about 30 minutes. This is not always possible at work, but if you have your own office, lock the door and don't answer the phone or your mobile. Sit in a comfortable position, reclining if at all possible, or lie on your back and close your eyes. Relax for about six seconds.

One after the other, tense a set of muscles and then relax them. The tensing should last for five, six or seven seconds, and the relaxation of the muscles should last for about 30 seconds. After the relaxation of each muscle, draw a deep breath. In turn, tense and relax your hands, arms, shoulders, head, eyes, chest, stomach, buttocks, legs and toes.

Because you are going through groups of muscles in turn, tensing and then releasing the tension, you can achieve deeper-than-normal levels of muscle relaxation. You will also obtain a better state of calmness. Although it will take you a little while to master the technique, after a short time you will be able to concentrate on specific muscle groups that you want to affect and you will take far less time to complete the exercise.

45. Use visualisation to help you cope with stress

Wouldn't it be nice if you were in a lovely place with no stress to affect you? You should try visualisation. Visualisation (sometimes called mental imagery) is a technique that slows you down and allows you to become quiet, mentally and physically. You imagine yourself in a warm, quiet place, and you feel calm and relaxed. You'll have to practise this technique before you encounter stress at work and then you can use it when you need.

How do you do it?

 Find a quiet place and sit down in a comfortable position.

 Close your eyes.

 Keep silent for ten seconds.

 Visualise yourself in your favourite place – it could be on a grassy mountainside, in a meadow, watching a beautiful sunset – we'll imagine you're on holiday, walking on an idyllic beach.

 You have no cares, worries or concerns.

 It is warm, the sun is shining and the beach is almost deserted.

 All you can hear is the gentle lapping of the waves from the blue, calm, ocean.

 You sit down on the sand and then you stretch out.

 You can feel the warmth of the sun on your skin and the soft sand under your body.

 You are totally relaxed and quiet (if you want you can have a gin and tonic in one hand).

 You lie there for a few minutes, enjoying the quiet and calm.

You then stand up and slowly walk off the beach.

You feel the warm sand under your feet, and you now are relaxed, at peace, quiet and revitalised.

You slowly open your eyes and return to the situation you are in – but this time you are better prepared to deal with events.

You can imagine anything you want – the only constraint is your own imagination. You can conjure up anything – it's not too hot, it's perfectly quiet, there are no flies to bother you, you feel completely safe – the environment is perfect. The only requirement is that the scene you are imagining helps you to relax.

Does visualisation work?

Most of the top sportsmen and women use visualisation techniques in their training and in competition. For example, before they play a shot, many elite golfers visualise how they will play the shot and where it will land. Athletes also use imagery to improve their performance. Try it at work; there are lots of tapes and CDs on sale to help you refine your technique.

46. How an employee assistance programme (EAP) can help you to manage your stress

When you're stressed and think it might be your work, home life or lifestyle that is causing the stress (but you're not sure), contact your organisation's employee assistance programme (EAP). If your company doesn't have one then you should press for one to be arranged. This is a resource that will need the support of the HR department, the trade unions that operate in your organisation or the people in charge. Other employees might also want to have access to such a resource.

What is an EAP?

Originally EAPs were set up in the USA in the 1940s to help employees who had alcohol problems. They expanded to include most health-related problems suffered by those at work, as well as stress problems that can occur at work. Subsequently, EAPs were used to help employees and their families who were affected in any way by stress and other events, such as personal or relationship issues, looking after aged parents, childcare and parenting issues, harassment at work, substance abuse, the work–life balance, financial or legal issues, and violence within the family. So, as you can see, they have broadened their coverage since they were established. In fact, a study of what EAPs do has been carried out and EAPs included topics such as assistance with severe medical conditions and those suffering from long-term illnesses, demotion, divorce, gambling, goal setting, job training, physical fitness, racial harassment, relocation, smoking, vocational guidance and weight control. Of course, not all of these are work related.

If an organisation uses an EAP it can either have its own programme in-house, and you would contact the EAP if you have a problem you want them to consider, or they use an EAP that is external to the company. In the case of the latter, you would be given a card with a phone number to contact. In both cases, information is strictly anonymous so no one from your company would know you have been in touch with the EAP. At least that's the theory. Of course, if the EAP is located in-house and the EAP office is in a room within the organisation, then you might be seen going in to their office.

So, if you have an EAP, use it if you need. If you don't have an EAP, try to convince your organisation that they need one – it could save the company money by reducing time off work, staff turnover, improving performance, etc.

47. Use neuro-linguistic programming (NLP) and cognitive behavioural therapy (CBT) to manage your stress

Neuro-linguistic programming (NLP)

NLP is based on the proposition that we create stress by our perceptions and beliefs about events rather than by the events themselves. NLP can change your perceptions from negative to positive, can change your beliefs about what is possible and can improve your performance. The techniques of NLP also allow you to overcome fears, mental blocks or emotional barriers, so that you can realise your potential. It can also improve your leadership abilities – whether you're trying to convince others to follow your ideas or you're in a position of leadership. It can change the way you speak, write and behave.

What is neuro-linguistic programming? Well, 'neuro' is how our brains and bodies work and 'linguistic' is how we convert all the things we experience – for instance, our feelings, what we see, what we hear – into words. But words are limited. 'Programming' is about the way we have programmed ourselves (perhaps badly) to deal with everything in our lives. NLP attempts to change the way you think and behave, and can help you to communicate more effectively with others.

There are lots of books and tapes and CDs that will introduce you to NLP. You can also attend a course on NLP, where you will learn techniques to change the ways in which you think and behave, and, more importantly, to deal with any stressors at work (which are usually people). You can also get in touch with someone who has recognised qualifications in NLP.

Cognitive behavioural therapy (CBT)

Some people believe cognitive behavioural therapy (CBT) is the most effective way to reduce stress. But you have to learn how to use CBT in advance, so that when you are faced with a stressful event you can use it to reduce or even to eliminate the stress to which you would otherwise be subjected. CBT can help employees with common workplace problems such as stress, anxiety and depression, and post-traumatic stress disorder. It can also be useful if you get angry very quickly or have a low opinion of yourself.

CBT involves identifying the sources of stress that may affect you, restructuring your priorities, altering the way in which you typically react to stress, and then determining the ways in which you can reduce and manage stress.

How does CBT work? Basically, CBT is a talking therapy. The Royal College of Psychiatrists in the UK suggests you meet with a qualified therapist every week or fortnight to undergo a 30- to 60-minute session. For the first few sessions the therapist ensures you are up to using CBT. You will be asked questions about your past life and then agree with the therapist what you want to deal with in the short, medium and long term. You will take a problem that is causing you stress at work and, with the help of the therapist, examine your thoughts, feelings and behaviours about the problem. With the therapist's help you will determine if these reactions are unrealistic or unhelpful, how they affect each other and how they affect you. You will then work to change your unhelpful thoughts and behaviours, and the therapist will ask you to make the changes to which you have agreed. At each subsequent meeting you discuss what you have done. After the course is completed you will be able to use the skills you now have when you need.

It has been found that CBT training provided by specialists and occupational health care staff (the latter could send emails to employees about CBT) reduces depression in employees. It has also been suggested that CBT is well suited to computerisation. For instance, a project was carried out to evaluate the effect of a computerised cognitive behavioural therapy programme aimed at emotionally distressed employees who had been absent from work with stress-related problems. This method helped the psychological recovery of these employees.

You can ask your organisation if they have a CBT specialist, or you can use a private therapist (although this will cost you money). Remember you must be able to use CBT before you try to use this technique with a stressful situation.

48. How to improve your time management

Someone once said time management courses are a waste of time. But, if you believe you are poor at managing your time at work, you might benefit from learning the basic principles. Time management can help you to deal with the stresses of work and cope with the strains of the workplace. Perhaps you find your time is 'robbed by time thieves' – the most important of these are:

◱ You are totally disorganised.

◱ You don't know what your goals are.

◱ You don't have a plan of work for the day.

◱ Anyone can come into your room or your workspace.

◱ You do not prioritise your work.

◱ You just can't say 'no' to anyone at work.

◱ You have a tendency to procrastinate.

◱ Your work is often interrupted by the phone, emails, messages, etc.

◱ You attend meaningless meetings.

Time management is fundamentally achieved by four major tasks that you will have to do in advance.

1. Make a list of all the activities you have to do in the coming day.

2. Prioritise these activities depending on their importance and urgency.

3. Make a schedule of the priorities you have produced.

4. Do the tasks that demand the most when you are at your best. For this you need to know when you are at your best mentally.

Of course, you may be doing a job that means your time is controlled by other people, for example if you are working on a machine or at a retailer's checkout. You may be unable to reorganise your job. So courses concerned with time management are mainly aimed at managing the stress of white-collar and management staff.

The sorts of things you can do in addition to the four major tasks outlined above are

○ Keep a log of how you spend your time. You can then examine where your time at work goes and may find you are doing things that are not important to you or to the organisation.

○ Improve your management of meetings. For instance, set an agenda and stick to it, give each item a time for discussion, and tell those at the meeting you'll be sticking to the time and agenda. When individuals drift off on a tangent and introduce something that is not relevant to the meeting, say the topic needs to be discussed at a separate or future meeting (or introduced under any other business). You can also suggest that a discussion of the topic (if you consider it important enough) should be scheduled to allow you to discuss it in more depth.

○ Delegate as many activities as and when you can. Don't 'dump' work on a colleague; find the right person to do the activity and give them any authority they need. Ensure that the person knows exactly what is wanted and by when; take their ideas on board and ask them what they think. Remember, you are ultimately the responsible person.

○ Block time – ensure your office door is closed, you will not be interrupted and you can get on with working as you please.

Remember the '80–20 rule' (the Pareto principle, named after the Italian economist Vilfredo Pareto). This principle says 80 per cent of the effort you expend at work provides 20 per cent of results, and the remaining 20 per cent of your effort supplies 80 per cent of your results. So concentrate on reducing the amount of time you spent on the former.

To determine if you have good time management skills, answer the following seven questions using this key:

1 = All the time

2 = Often

3 = Sometimes

4 = Rarely

5 = Never

1. Do you find you have to rush tasks?

2. Do you leave many activities unfinished because you don't like them?

3. Do you waste a lot of time?

4. Do you miss a lot of deadlines?

5. Do you feel you have insufficient time to relax?

6. Do you feel upset by the quality and quantity of work you have to do?

7. Do you have to do work you feel you shouldn't be doing?

Add the scores for each question.

If you scored between 7 and 14 you have plenty of scope to improve your performance by bettering your time management.

If you scored between 15 and 27 you can improve your time management, which at present is so-so.

If you scored between 28 and 35 your time management skills are good.

49. How you can increase your resilience at work

Dean Becker wrote in the *Harvard Business Review* that 'more than education, more than experience, more than training, a person's level of resilience will determine who succeeds and who fails. That's true in the cancer ward, it's true in the Olympics, and it's true in the boardroom.' It's also true in the workplace for the employee who is not at board level but has to do what may be a boring, demanding job every day.

Do you have resilience? First of all, we had better define what we mean by resilience. It's your ability to 'bounce back' from stress and adverse events, and to cope with unpleasant circumstances at work, such as a poor performance review, too much work, making mistakes, missing out on a promotion, etc. There are two things that contribute to resilience. Your personality, which may mean you are naturally a resilient person; and support from other people or organisations (such as a voluntary organisation or a religious community), which may be in the form of emotional, financial or psychological support. Once you reach adulthood it's quite difficult to change your personality, so if you are naturally resilient you may be knocked down by what happens to you at work, but you come back stronger than ever and learn from what's happened to you. But many people are not naturally resilient. You can improve your resilience – it will take time, but it can be done. The UK National Health Service believes there are ten ways in which you can build up your emotional resilience.

1. Talk to someone about your feelings – it could be a friend, a family member, a counsellor, etc.

2. Improve your self-esteem, what you think of yourself. Lack of self-esteem can be detrimental. Treat yourself as you would treat a valued friend. Notice when you're putting yourself down, such as 'you're so stupid for not getting that job' and think 'would I say that to my best friend?' – you probably wouldn't. There are lots of resources to help you improve your self-esteem, including books, CDs, DVDs and articles on the Internet.

3. Keep your stress levels as low as is possible, by using some of the advice in this book.

4. Enjoy yourself. This can involve anything that gives you a boost, something you like or are good at.

5. Limit your alcohol intake.

6. Stick to a well-balanced diet.

7. Do plenty of exercise.

8. Get enough sleep.

9. Develop good relationships at work. Consider how you can improve your relationships, for instance, listen to others, don't judge them, help your colleagues and read the section in this book about how to get on with your colleagues.

10. Know the warning signs that you are under stress. These could include suffering from racing thoughts, feeling overwhelmed, suffering from aches and pains, eating more or less than usual, etc.

By yourself, you can achieve most of the goals on the list. If you are unsure how to accomplish any of them, ask a colleague, friend or family member.

Complete a questionnaire that will indicate your level of resilience. A free questionnaire has been developed by Robertson Cooper, a company that promotes the benefits and methods of achieving employee well-being. You'll find details at www.robertsoncooper. com/iresilience. The questionnaire, which you complete online, will take about 20 minutes and is based on the four key components of resilience – confidence, adaptability, purposefulness and social support. You will receive an online report to show which of the four key areas you naturally draw on for your resilience and it then relates these to common workplace situations, to provide clear and concise feedback on how to improve your resilience. Some of the questions you will be asked are shown below. You answer each question in one of five ways. You can choose to strongly disagree, disagree, remain neutral, agree or strongly agree.

I consider myself broad minded and tolerant of other people's lifestyles.

I am determined to succeed.

I think of myself as a shy person.

I prefer working on my own.

I rarely feel discouraged by events.

I often feel bad about the way things have turned out.

I try to do jobs carefully, so they won't have to be done again.

I believe it's foolish to trust people before you know them well.

I find that taking an indirect approach is often the best way to get what I want from people.

I get annoyed easily.

A study carried out by the University of California, San Francisco, says you should try to increase your resilience by developing a personal strategy using these guidelines:

 Take care of yourself.

 Establish and maintain connections.

 Monitor your exposure to media coverage of violence.

 Avoid viewing problems as impossible.

 Accept changes as part of life.

 Progress towards your goal.

 Take clear actions.

Maintain a hopeful outlook.

 Keep things in perspective and avoid 'catastrophising'.

Nurture a positive view of yourself.

Engage in opportunities of self-discovery.

Improve your resilience to cope with whatever work (and life) throws at you.

50. How to motivate yourself

Sometimes it's a struggle to keep yourself motivated. You might be stressed by your lack of drive. You are anxious, depressed, and uncertain about your future and the future of the work you are doing. Is there anything you can do to invigorate yourself, to increase your motivation and reduce the stress caused by your lack of motivation? Because self-motivation is so important, this book will spend some time on the topic. One way you can increase your self-motivation is to take the self-motivation quiz below (produced and copyrighted by Mind Tools and available at www.mindtools.com/pages/article/newLDR_57.htm) in an attempt to find out why you are so unmotivated or demotivated.

For each of the 12 statements, give a score that best describes you, using the following scale:

1 = Not at all

2 = Rarely

3 = Sometimes

4 = Often

5 = Very often

Please answer questions as you actually are (rather than how you think you should be), and don't worry if some questions seem to score in the 'wrong direction'.

1. I'm unsure of my ability to achieve the goals I set for myself.

2. When working on my goals, I put in maximum effort and work even harder if I've suffered a setback.

3. I regularly set goals and objectives to achieve my vision for my life.

4. I think positively about setting goals and making sure my needs are met.

5. I use rewards (and consequences) to keep myself focused. For example, if I finish my report on time, I allow myself to take a coffee break.

6. I believe that if I work hard and apply my abilities and talents, I will be successful.

7. I worry about deadlines and getting things done, which causes stress and anxiety.

8. When an unexpected event threatens or jeopardises my goal, I can tend to walk away, set a different goal, and move in a new direction.

9. My biggest reward after completing something is the satisfaction of knowing I've done a good job.

10. I tend to do the minimum amount of work necessary to keep my boss and my team satisfied.

11. I tend to worry about why I won't reach my goals, and I often focus on why something probably won't work.

12. I create a vivid and powerful vision of my future success before embarking on a new goal.

© Mind Tools Ltd, 1996–2012. Reproduced with permission.

When you are finished, add the figures you gave, remembering that questions 1, 7, 10 and 11 are reverse-scored (so subtract your original score from 6).

What does your score mean?

If you scored 44 to 60 – wonderful! You get things done and you don't let anything stand in your way. You make a conscious effort to stay self-motivated, and you spend significant time and effort on setting goals and acting to achieve those goals. You attract and inspire others with your success. Treasure this – and be aware that not everyone is as self-motivated as you are!

If you scored 28 to 43 – you're doing OK on self-motivation. You're certainly not failing – however, you could achieve much more. To achieve what you want, try to increase the motivational factors in all areas of your life.

If you scored 12 to 27 – you allow your personal doubts and fears to keep you from succeeding. You've probably had a few incomplete goals in the past, so you may have convinced yourself that you aren't self-motivated – and then you've made that come true. Break this harmful pattern now, and start believing in yourself again.

So, if you want to increase your self-motivation, what can you do? Here are some of the things recommended by Mind Tools. Self-motivation is complex. It's linked to your level of initiative in setting challenging goals for yourself; your belief that you have the skills and abilities needed to achieve those goals; and your expectation that if you put in enough hard work, you will succeed (or at least be in the running, if it's a competitive situation). Four factors are necessary to build the strongest levels of self-motivation:

 Self-confidence and self-efficacy.

 Positive thinking and positive thinking about the future.

Focus and strong goals.

A motivating environment.

By working on all of these together, you should quickly improve your self-motivation. Let's look at each of these factors individually.

To improve your self-confidence and self-efficacy (found in statements 1, 2, 6 and 8 above) take these steps:

 Think about the achievements in your life.

Examine your strengths to understand what you can build on.

Determine what other people see as your strengths and key capabilities.

 Set achievable goals for yourself, work to achieve them and enjoy that achievement.

 Seek out mentors and other people who model the competencies, skills and attributes you desire.

To increase your positive thinking, and positive thinking about the future (found in statements 4, 9, 11 and 12 above):

 Become aware of your thoughts. Write these down throughout the day.

 Challenge your negative thoughts and replace them with positive ones.

 Create a strong and vivid picture of what it will be like to achieve your goals.

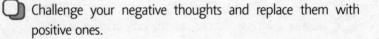 Develop affirmations or statements that you can repeat to yourself throughout the day. These statements should remind you of what you want to achieve and why you will achieve it.

Practise positive thinking until you automatically think about yourself and the world in a positive way, every day.

To improve your focus and set strong goals (found in statements 3 and 7 above), adopt the following:

Clarity – effective goals are clear, measurable, specific and based on behaviour, not outcomes.

Challenge – goals should be difficult enough to be interesting, but not so difficult that you can't reach them.

Commitment – goals should be attainable and relevant. They should contribute in a significant way to the major objectives that you're trying to achieve.

Regularity of feedback – monitor your progress towards your goals regularly to maintain your sense of momentum and enthusiasm, and enjoy your progress towards those goals.

Sufficient respect for complexity – if the goal involves complex work, make sure you don't over-commit. Complex work can take an unpredictably long time to complete (particularly if you have to learn how to do the task 'on the job').

To make yours a motivating environment (found in statements 5 and 10 above):

 Look for teamwork opportunities. Working in a team makes you accountable to others.

Ask your boss for specific targets and objectives to help you measure your success.

Ask for interesting assignments.

◯ Set up some goals that you can easily achieve. Quick wins are great for getting you motivated.

◯ Pair up with people you trust to be supportive and ask them to help keep you accountable.

◯ Try not to work by yourself too much. Balance the amount of time you work from home with time spent working with others.

Improving your self-motivation is not easy, but if you follow the items outlined above, you can do it!

Body boost

When you are stressed your body's needs change. Zinc is required for normal immune function and when you are stressed your body requires more of it. On the other hand you may be drinking more caffeine and alcohol to cope with your stress. These both disrupt your sleep patterns and create short-term mood-boosts, leaving your body craving more when the effects wear off. In times of stress, consider reducing your intake of both drinks.

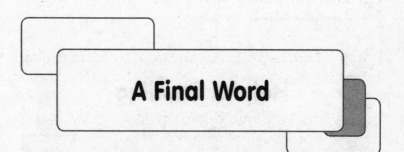

A Final Word

If you're suffering from stress at work there are numerous actions you can take. In the end, it's up to you what you want to do. However, you should always let your boss/organisation/trade union/staff representative/human resources department know that you are suffering from stress and tell them about anything that might help to eliminate the stress. In the end you may have to accept there will always be stress at work and you'll need to find ways to reduce your stress levels either at work or at home. We've also shown the changes that your boss and management can make. Stress at work can be managed and reduced, if not eliminated.

Helpful Reading

Here are some books that you might want to read. You'll get more information from them about stress at work and how it can be managed.

Cooper, C L, Holdsworth, L and Johnson, S, *Organisational Behaviour for Dummies* (John Wiley & Sons, 2012). This book looks at everything related to individual and group behaviour at work and the effects they have on the organisation.

Robertson, I and Cooper, C L, *Well-being: Productivity and Happiness at Work* (Palgrave Macmillan, 2011). The authors have carried out a major study that indicates high levels of psychological well-being among employees will mean lower sickness-absence levels, attraction and retention of talented people, and more satisfied customers, clients or service users. It suggests ways in which organisations can provide their employees with high levels of psychological well-being.

Schafer, W, *Stress Management for Wellness* (fourth edition, Wadsworth Publishing Company, 1999). This book is ideal for students at college or university.

Theobald, T and Cooper, C L, *Doing the Right Thing: The Importance of Wellbeing in the Workplace* (Palgrave Macmillan, 2012). This book gives answers to stressful situations at work and provides sound strategies for a more harmonious workplace.

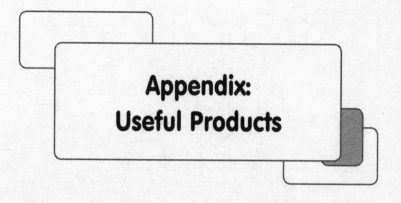

Appendix:
Useful Products

There are also CDs and DVDs you can use to help reduce and manage your stress levels.

Rachael Eccles has produced many useful CDs and MP3s, among them *Self Hypnosis – Stop Anxiety, Self Hypnosis – Anger Management,* and *Self Hypnosis - Giving a Presentation.*

Howell, Maggie, *Relaxation and Stress Management* (Natal Hypnotherapy, 2005).

McManus, Carolyn, *Progressive Relaxation & Autogenic Training* (CD Baby, 2012).

NOTES

NOTES

FREE
YOUR
Back

**Ease pain and regain
natural poise with gentle
exercises based on the
Alexander Technique**

Penny Ingham
&
Colin Shelbourn

Free Your Back

Ease pain and regain natural poise with gentle exercises based
on the Alexander Technique

Penny Ingham & Colin Shelbourn

ISBN: 978 1 84957 378 2   Paperback   £9.99

First developed by Frederick Alexander in 1890, the Alexander
technique retrains the body to work in a more economical and less
stressful way, and can be used for improved breathing and joint
mobility, and staying calm under pressure.

This practical book offers easy and effective solutions to posture
problems at home and at work, with illustrated exercises to help you
break bad habits and learn to let your body relax.

Free Your Back will change the way you stand, walk and sit. The advice
will help you to ease those painful stiff necks and backaches and allow
you freer movement and better balance throughout your body, for a
healthier life free of back pain.

50 things you can do today to manage
stress

Wendy Green

Foreword by Jenny Edwards,
Vice Chair of the International Stress Management Association UK
and Editor of Stress News

PERSONAL HEALTH GUIDES

50 Things You Can Do Today To Manage Stress

Wendy Green

ISBN: 978 1 84957 202 0   Paperback   £6.99

In this reassuring and easy-to-follow book, Wendy Green explains the psychological and lifestyle factors that contribute to stress and offers practical advice and a holistic approach to help you deal with its symptoms, including simple dietary and lifestyle changes and DIY complementary therapies. Find out 50 things you can do today to help you manage stress, including:

- Identify your stress triggers and understand how stress affects you
- Simplify your life by de-junking your home and taking control of your spending
- Introduce regular exercise at a pace that suits you to reduce stress levels
- Adopt an anti-stress attitude by living in the moment
- Choose beneficial foods and supplements
- Reduce stress in your daily life through aromatherapy and homeopathy
- Find helpful organisations and products